Marcella Gerrard's Galway estate, 1820–70

GW00801838

Maynooth Studies in Local History

SERIES EDITOR Raymond Gillespie

This volume is one of six Maynooth studies in local history published this year. Like the hundred or so that have preceded them, each has a task that is deceptively simple: to reconstruct and explain something of the realities of the local worlds that made up Ireland in the past. The apparent simplicity of this task conceals the considerable complexity and diversity of local societies that are revealed in these small books. Those local societies are not simply the expression of administrative units or geographical regions but social worlds that were carefully crafted and maintained in Ireland over time. That process of making local societies was one in which people interacted within their own spaces to create structures that made life workable on a day-to-day basis. They found common cause to hold together their local worlds but also sources of conflict that would sometimes drive them apart, as in 1916 when some communities were riven apart by violence and insurrection. The story of Skerries' involvement in 1916 provides a perspective on the contingent local processes in what is often seen as a purely national event. In the process of shaping local worlds people placed their own stamp on the things that they used to make daily life possible. Furniture and fittings in Borris House, for instance, reveal much about local perceptions of fashion and sociability and the role of women as architects in early nineteenth-century Ireland provides a distinctive insight into how spaces were ordered for living. Other sorts of local worlds were shaped in other ways. Estates had the potential to be the building blocks of local societies but often landlord priorities and those of the tenantry diverged, even when they had other features in common, as in the Gerrard estate in Galway. Elsewhere, large industrial operations, such as the Portmarnock Brick Works, might provide the basis of local societies. In the case of Dublin's South Circular Road people not only of diverse socio-economic backgrounds but also of different ethnic and religious origins were thrown together as a new suburb was created. At street corners and in churches they found ways to make local society work in a potentially divisive world threatened by the tensions leading up to the First World War.

Like previous titles in this series these small books recover the socially diverse worlds of urban and rural dwellers, men as well as women, and the rich occupants of great houses and evicted tenants. They often inhabited worlds that were little affected by the themes of national history, though that larger story often did impinge on their lives. Reconstructing those experiences is one of the challenges at the forefront of Irish historical research, and, in their own way, these studies convey the vibrancy and excitement of exploring the local past on its own terms.

Maynooth Studies in Local History: Number 107

Marcella Gerrard's Galway estate, 1820–70
'Awful Extermination of Tenantry'

Tom Crehan

FOUR COURTS PRESS

Set in 10pt on 12pt Bembo *by*
Carrigboy Typesetting Services *for*
FOUR COURTS PRESS LTD
7 Malpas Street, Dublin 8, Ireland
www.fourcourtspress.ie
and in North America for
FOUR COURTS PRESS
c/o ISBS, 920 N.E. 58th Avenue, Suite 300, Portland, OR 97213.

ISBN 978–1–84682–401–2

Printed in Ireland
by SprintPrint, Dublin.

Contents

	Acknowledgments	6
	Introduction	7
1	A gathering storm	12
2	'Awful extermination of tenantry'	22
3	An uncontrollable fancy for pasture	34
4	The post-Famine years	45
	Conclusion	56
	APPENDIX 1. Householders evicted at Ballinlass, 13 March 1846	59
	APPENDIX 2. Householders evicted at Connor/Corner village, November 1848	60
	Notes	61

FIGURES

1	Location map of Gerrard estate	10
2	Newspaper notice, Michael O'Connor	26
3	Local monument commemorating Ballinlass evictions	33
4	Line drawing of Netterville Lodge	54

TABLES

1.1	Population of the parishes of Ballynakill and Killian, 1821–41	15
3.1	Gerrard landholdings in Ballynakill and Killian parishes, 1854	39
3.2	Population of Gerrard landholdings in Ballynakill and Killian parishes, 1841–61	41
3.3	Number of houses on Gerrard landholdings in Ballynakill and Killian, 1841–61	42

Acknowledgments

I would like to acknowledge, with gratitude, the following people for their help and support in the preparation of this work. My MA thesis supervisor, Dr Gerard P. Moran, has been an inspirational figure who provided support, guidance and gentle criticism as required. His knowledge of the period and the issues involved provided me with a wealth of expertise which was generously shared. I would also like to thank the History Department of NUI Maynooth, and in particular Professor Raymond Gillespie for the opportunity to contribute to this series.

I am grateful for the cooperation of the various institutions which facilitated my research. The library at NUI Maynooth, the National Library of Ireland, National Archives of Ireland, library of the Royal Irish Academy, the Registry of Deeds and the archives section of Galway County Library were helpful and accommodating in the provision of research material. Robert Grace was of great assistance in the preparation of a location map, James H. Cornell generously permitted the use of his drawing of Netterville Lodge and David Walsh kindly supplied a photograph of the Ballinlass monument.

Finally, I would like to thank Angela Crehan for her forbearance, support and, on occasions, tolerance in my pursuit of this project.

Introduction

The first half of the 19th century was a time of social, political and economic upheaval for Ireland. At the beginning of the century it is estimated that the country had a population of nearly five-and-a-half million people. By 1841 this had increased to more than eight million before falling to six-and-a-half million by 1851. The rapid population increase in the years 1800 to 1841 led to an enormous demand for land and a consequential increase in rents, until there were simply too many people attempting to gain a living on too little land. Many landlords, especially those who resided on their estates, committed themselves to improvements. For some, improvements meant the draining and reclamation of bogs and marginal land, as well as attempting to improve fertility by the addition of fertiliser and the practice of crop rotation. Additionally, landlords such as the earl of Clancarty at Garbally Park, near Ballinasloe, were instrumental in the setting up of agricultural societies and model farms to encourage innovative agricultural methods. Two major impediments to innovation were the small size of many holdings and the rundale system of landholding. The census of 1841 indicated that 75 per cent of land holdings were less than five acres. In addition, the rundale, or 'village' system meant that many farms were held in a common system by groups of tenants, one of them being the head tenant who decided how the land was to be divided out among members of the group. In practice this resulted in a patchwork of land allocations often without fences or mearings of any kind. The conversion of a landed estate into larger holdings inevitably meant fewer tenants and presented the problem of how to deal with those tenants who were surplus to requirements.

This short book examines such a landed estate in east Galway, though the purpose of its owner was not to create larger holdings for letting to fewer tenants. Rather it was to convert a landed estate into a grazing farm, with its owner a farmer rather than a landlord. In 1822, on his marriage to the estate's owner, Marcella Netterville, John Gerrard of Gibbstown, Co. Meath became the beneficial owner of an estate of approximately 7,000 acres in east Galway. He set about converting it into a huge grazing farm in order to maximize land productivity at a minimum labour cost. In order to achieve this, he first had to dismantle the existing tenant framework, with its attendant problems of over-population, traditional practices of subdivision, and the rundale method of sharing tracts of rented land by groups of tenants. The period 1822–70 allows the activities of John and Marcella Gerrard to be examined in a national context of the considerable number of similar land clearances before, during and after the Famine, especially in the years 1845–53. The available evidence suggests that the Gerrard clearances began as early as 1840, well in advance of the Famine, and continued unabated through the Famine years.

The estate was located in the north eastern portion of Co. Galway on the western basin of the river Suck. The town of Ballinasloe is some 20 miles to the east while Tuam is a similar distance to the west. The town of Roscommon is approximately 15 miles to the south. The nearest market towns are Mount Bellew, 5 miles to the south west, and Ballygar, a similar distance to the north east. The terrain is low-lying with a mixture of arable farmland and a good deal of bogland.

The topic of landlord-tenant relationships in the period in question has received considerable attention from historians, particularly in the last 20 years. In *Graziers, land reform, and political conflict in Ireland*, David Seth Jones examines the role of graziers in the agricultural and tenurial changes which took place in Ireland in the early 19th century.[1] In *Landlords and tenants in mid-Victorian Ireland*, W.E. Vaughan offers a critical insight into the interaction between landlord and tenant in the post-Famine period.[2] Tim P. O'Neill has written extensively on evictions before and during the Famine and has offered the view that 'the underestimation of eviction rates and even threats of eviction has led to a distortion of Famine studies by a generation of historians.'[3] James S. Donnelly has examined the impact of the Great Famine on the fragile relationship between landlord and tenant in that crucial period, noting that by a combination of clearances, mass emigration and famine, 'Irish landowners were able to achieve their long-desired objective of the consolidation of holdings on a large scale.'[4] One of the many solutions offered to alleviate the large population and scarcity of rented land was the facilitation of emigration to the United States and Canada. In *Sending out Ireland's poor*, Gerard Moran explores the assisted emigration schemes, beginning with the Robinson scheme which oversaw the emigration of two consignments of migrants from Cork in 1823 and 1825. Robinson, a member of the Canadian legislative assembly, visited Cork and personally selected the prospective *émigrés*, having to 'walk a fine line with his selections; the landed proprietors wanted their troublesome and pauperized tenants to be assisted while Robinson realized that only good and industrious tenants should be sent.'[5] Gerard Moran has also examined the estate management of Sir Robert Gore Booth in the years 1814 to 1876. Moran pays particular attention to the assisted emigration schemes sponsored by Sir Robert in his efforts to improve the estate by 'striping' it into larger holdings with the resultant surplus tenantry.[6] Liam Dolan has conducted a detailed examination of the eviction process in his study of the clearances carried out by John George Adair at Derryveagh in Co. Donegal in 1861. Although these clearances took place somewhat later than the Gerrard clearances, they are worthy of comparison in that the Derryveagh tenants feared that they were to be replaced by grazing sheep tended by a small group of shepherds recruited in Scotland.[7] Another comprehensive study on evictions has been provided by Gerard Moran who deals with the conflict between the landlord, Bishop Thomas Plunkett, and the tenants at Partry, Co. Mayo, led by their Catholic curate, Fr Patrick Lavelle.[8] Again these events occurred later than the Gerrard clearances. Yet they have some resonances with the Gerrard clearances in that ostensibly they were about the breach of conditions of lease but in reality were about an entirely different matter, namely the competition for souls between the Catholic and Established churches. Two studies relating to the Bellew estate at Mount Bellew, Co. Galway provided valuable historical background. Karen Harvey's examination of the Bellew family, Catholic neighbours of the Netterville family, offers an insight into the challenges faced by the families transplanted to Connacht in the 17th century, and their subsequent integration into the gentry families of Galway.[9] Joe Clarke's study of the improvements undertaken by Sir Christopher Dillon Bellew in the late 18th and early 19th centuries sheds considerable light on the estate management practices at that crucial period.[10] Jim Gilligan has examined the world of the Meath grazier in the latter half of the 19th century. Although his time frame is somewhat later than John Gerrard's, his study provides a useful insight into the practices of Edward Delaney and other graziers who were almost contemporaneous with John Gerrard. Anne Coleman has explored the topic of social unrest in Roscommon during the 1840s. As the Gerrard estate was some 10 miles from the southern part of Co. Roscommon, her findings have some relevance. She notes the cost of land rental, particularly conacre, was a cause of social unrest but 'unrest in the county did not suddenly cease but the capacity of the poor to resist was eroded as starvation took its toll in 1846.'[11]

The absence to date of any relevant estate records is a drawback. However the contemporary newspapers, provincial, national and international, provided a rich vein of reportage and comment on the evictions at Ballinlass in March 1846, and subsequent clearances at Connor (Corner) village and Kilcoosh. Government papers such as the *Devon Commission*, census reports, land valuation, notification of evictions and Hansard recording of debates in both houses of parliament were also fertile sources of information. This study draws upon a range of contemporary writings such as Arthur Young's *Tour of Ireland*,[12] Samuel Lewis' *Topographical dictionary*[13] and S. Redmond's pamphlet, *Landlordism in Ireland*, comprising the reports submitted to the *Freeman's Journal* in the immediate aftermath of the clearances at Ballinlass.[14] The marriage settlement of John Gerrard and Marcella Netterville as well as the will of her grandfather Edmond Netterville shed valuable light on the ownership of the estate and led to a greater insight into the dispute which followed her death in 1865.

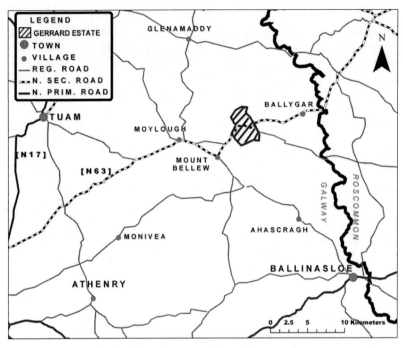

1 Location map of Gerrard estate.

The first chapter examines the background of the Catholic Netterville
family and their banishment from Dowth to the parish of Killian, barony of
Killian, east Galway, in the 17th century. The will and codicil of Edmond
Netterville in 1765–77, following the indiscretions of his son Frederick, were
to have a far-reaching impact on the future of the estate. Similarly the marriage
of his granddaughter Marcella Netterville to John Gerrard of Gibbstown, Co.
Meath, in 1822, signalled a significant change in the management of the estate.
The second chapter focuses on the estate management of John Gerrard and
his policy of clearing his lands of tenants in order to further the grazing of
cattle, a practice which had served him well in his Gibbstown estate. Particular
attention is paid to the evictions in the townland of Ballinlass in March 1846.
The widespread newspaper coverage of these evictions propelled Ballinlass
onto the national and international stage and elicited a detailed response from
John Gerrard. This response served to re-ignite the newspaper coverage,
highlighting the growing influence of newspapers, provincial and national,
among an increasingly literate society. The third chapter examines the aftermath of the Ballinlass evictions. It examines the newspaper and parliamentary
coverage at home and abroad as well as the editorial stances adopted by the
various newspapers. This chapter also examines the continuation of the

landlord's clearance policy despite the widespread negative publicity which his actions generated. Chapter three also utilizes data gleaned from the census reports of 1841–61 and Griffith's Valuation to analyse the effects of John Gerrard's clearance policy on his Galway estate. The final chapter outlines the events following the deaths of John Gerrard in 1858 and his wife Marcella in 1865. It goes on to describe the competition for ownership of the estate and its eventual division among three aspirant owners. The chapter also discusses the possible fate of the many tenants who were dispossessed and had their dwellings destroyed.

Through the use of primary and secondary sources, this work hopes to present a micro-study of a landed estate, which, in conjunction with existing literature, will provide a greater understanding of the complex world of landlord-tenant relations in the first half of the 19th century. It presents an analysis of a landlord's local response to global economic issues and changes, and highlights the position of John Netterville Gerrard as one of the major instigators of eviction as a method of estate management before, during and after the Famine.

1. A gathering storm

The 17th century, beginning as it did with the battle of Kinsale and ending with the aftermath of the battle of the Boyne, had a profound and far-reaching impact on the Gaelic way of life. The Old English, the landed the aristocracy who traced their roots to Norman settlement, became integrated into Irish society in both law and status. The land confiscations which took place through the century meant that much of the land of Ireland changed hands. The Netterville family is a case in point. It is believed that they came to Ireland during the reign of Henry II and settled at Dowth, Co. Meath, where they appear to have prospered. Luke Netterville of Dowth was appointed one of the justices of the Court of Queen's Bench in Ireland on 15 October 1559.[1] His grandson Nicholas Netterville was raised to the peerage of Ireland on 3 April 1622 as Viscount Netterville of Dowth. Nicholas had four sons by his first wife, Eleanor Bathe. One of these sons, Patrick Netterville, was the founder of the Galway branch of the family. His father, Nicholas had married Mary Brice on the death of his first wife Eleanor. The family were caught up in the political maelstrom of the time and were transplanted to Connacht. The Books of Survey and Distribution indicate that Nicholas and Mary Netterville were granted 1,043 profitable acres in the parish of Killian, barony of Killian, in east Galway.[2] Some of the Dowth estates were subsequently restored to the family on the accession of Charles II to the throne. It is unclear if Nicholas and Mary Netterville actually claimed their grant of land in Connacht, but if they did not, their son Patrick certainly did. He settled at Leighcarrow (Lecarrow) in the parish of Killian and the family prospered by all accounts.

Patrick died in 1676 and was succeeded by his son, Nicholas, who married twice and had two families. The two families went in different directions and this was to become a factor in the subsequent claims for the title of Viscount Netterville. By this time the family had moved a short distance to the townland of Longford in the parish of Ballynakill, still in the barony of Killian. The estate next went to Patrick, son of Nicholas by his first wife, Dorothea Douglas, and subsequently to Patrick's son, Edmond Netterville, who acquired the estate in 1736. At some point, the family, like many of the transplants, renounced their Catholicism and become Protestant. It appears also that the rural tranquillity of east Galway may have lost its appeal to Edmond Netterville, as in his will dated 15 November 1765, he described himself as Edmond Netterville of Longford and Glasnevin. Furthermore, the will stipulated that his dearly

beloved wife Margery be granted 'the use of my plate, house, furniture, &
holding at Glasnevin from the time of my decease until my son can shall come
to the age of twenty-one years'.[3] He wisely added that the property would be
hers for her lifetime in the event of his son not reaching the age of 21 years.

This will of Edmond Netterville is of importance as it was to have profound
implications for the tenants of the entire estate some 70 years later. The will
and a subsequent codicil also indicate that Edmond was successful in enlarging
his estate. He referred to the lands at 'Carrownagappul and Ballenlass', which
he had purchased from neighbouring landlord Sir Patrick Bellew. The original
will is a fairly straightforward, if wordy, document in that it bequeathed his
estates 'to the use of my first and every other son & the heirs male of the body
or bodies of such sons, according to priority of birth, the elder of such son
and sons, and the heirs male of his body, always to be preferred to the younger,
and the heirs male of his body'.[4] The will then outlined a lengthy and detailed
order of inheritance in the event of such son or sons having no male offspring.
Subsequent events were to bring about a codicil to the will, which was added
on 11 April 1776.

Edmond Netterville and his wife Margery Trench of Garbally, Ballinasloe,
had two children, Frederick and Margery. It appears that Frederick, his heir,
was a rather colourful young man who had an active, if imprudent, social life.
He became involved with, and actually married, a notorious Dublin prostitute
known as Kitty Cut a Dash and also accumulated debts of several thousand
pounds. This was a huge embarrassment for the family and proved most
expensive to untangle. The marriage was dissolved in some way, but Kitty
proved to be a formidable negotiator and achieved a financial settlement of
£5,000.[5] In addition Edmond was forced to settle the debts of his hapless son.
Kitty, however, retained the name Netterville, and under the name Catherine
Netterville, remained a courtesan of repute and had a large residence in
Grafton Street. Edmond Netterville took swift and decisive action to curb the
activities of his errant son. He was instrumental in the marriage of Frederick
to a more respectable spouse named Mary Keogh of Portumna, and settled
them in Woodbrook House, on his Galway estate. The codicil to his will
stipulated that the residue of his estate be invested in government debentures
to provide a once-off payment to Frederick's children at their reaching 21
years of age. In the codicil he bluntly stated: 'it being my intention that the
said Fred[k] Nettervill shall receive no benefit from the said trust, as by his
improperly contracting debts, he has been the occasion of my family estate
being curtailed.'[6] Edmond Netterville died in 1777 and probate was granted
to Sir Samuel Bradstreet on 18 June of that year.[7] Frederick and his new wife
Mary Keogh had six children, Edmond, Robert, Frederick, Marcella, Cressy
and Maria. They appear to have lived in Woodbrook House for a only a short
time before returning to Glasnevin following the death of Edmond senior, as

the baptism records of the Church of Ireland in Glasnevin show the baptisms of Walter Robert Netterville on 7 May 1778 and Margery Netterville on 10 July 1779, both the children of Frederick and Mary Netterville.[8] This raises the question as to whether the infant baptized as Margery is one and the same person as the woman later known as Marcella. One piece of local oral history points in this direction. The older generation of people in the Killian area of east Galway, when talking about the evictions, still refer to Mrs Gerrard as 'Madge', perhaps indicating that Margery and Marcella are indeed the same person. In any event, it appears that from the end of the 18th century the Netterville lands in east Galway were administered from afar. The absence of a resident landlord usually meant a lack of improvement or investment in the estate and as a consequence whatever difficulties were arising nationally between landlord and tenant were almost certain to have arisen on the Netterville estate.

While the estate may have been under remote administration in the early part of the 19th century, Ireland was undergoing major political, social and economic change. In the world of politics, the new century heralded in the Act of Union. This abolished the Irish parliament and brought the government of Ireland directly under the control of the British parliament in Westminster. 'Ireland was henceforth to be represented in the parliament of the United Kingdom in London by (a) twenty-eight Irish peers and four bishops in the House of Lords, and (b) one hundred MPs in the House of Commons.'[9] Ireland would contribute two-seventeenths of the total United Kingdom expenditure. The rebellion of 1798 had to a large extent polarised Irish society and a 'Protestant front had now clearly emerged, with security for Protestant lives and interests as its overriding object.'[10] Many Protestants opposed the Act of Union, believing that a Protestant parliament in Dublin was the most effective way to deliver this security; nevertheless the Union was passed after a second attempt, following months of persuasion and patronage. Emmet's rising in 1803, which in reality was the final gasp of the 1798 rising, effectively killed off Protestant opposition to the Union. While Emmet's failed rising, to some extent ended political discontent, it did not bring violence to an end.

> Rural Ireland, in the first half of the nineteenth century was to see a great deal of popular discontent, expressed in organised and often violent protest. The greatest part of this protest, however, was to be limited in its aims, concerned solely with economic grievances and seeking to defend what were seen as existing rights rather than to overthrow the existing social order.[11]

Groups such as Whiteboys, Threshers, Rickites and Ribbonmen epitomized this type of protest, which was mainly rural in character. These groups mainly concerned themselves with 'conacre, rents, labourers' wages, tithes, taxes and priests' dues; and participants seem to have been drawn almost exclusively from the poor having little or no land.'[12] The hopes of some Catholics that the Act of Union would improve their lot proved to be unfounded. Not only were they excluded from high office such as parliament, lord lieutenant and membership of the privy council, they were *de facto* excluded from offices for which they were theoretically eligible. 'Of 1,314 offices connected with the administration of justice to which Catholics could legally be appointed, only 39 were in fact held by Catholics.'[13] At local level, the organs of government such as magistrates and grand juries tended to be almost exclusively Protestant, often unsympathetic to the Catholic and frequently landless majority.

The 18th century was a time of comparative peace in Ireland, which allowed the economy to recover. Demand for agricultural produce grew. England's involvement in foreign wars ensured a steady demand for foodstuffs, particularly grain. In this regard Ó Tuathaigh observes, 'A continuously expanding demand in the British market and the attractions of high prices, particularly in the boom war years encouraged Irish farmers to increase their output.'[14] Better prices for crops meant more demand for land resulting in higher costs for land rental. The introduction of the potato in the previous century provided a cheap nutritious food that could be cultivated in poor quality ground. These combined factors contributed to a steady increase in population, which in turn created a greater demand for land.

A similar rise in population in England provided a ready market for Irish produce, especially foodstuffs. In the early part of the century, England was at war with France and this protracted war created demand for grain. This caused a change from pasture to the more labour intensive tillage, creating a demand for labour and also for land. The almost universal adoption of the potato as the staple diet of the poorer classes provided a high-yielding, nutritious food supply. By 1845 it is estimated that the population had reached 8.5 million.[15] This increase at national level is mirrored by population figures in the areas in question, as is indicated in table 1.1.

Table 1.1. Population of the parishes of Ballynakill and Killian, 1821–41

| | | Population | | |
Parish	Acreage	1821	1831	1841
Ballynakill	4,221	1,239	1,630	1,762
Killian	13,563	4,663	5,401	5,671

Source: Census of Ireland, 1821–41.

The figures bear some similarity to national figures. At a national level the population increase from 1821 to 1831 was of the order of 20 per cent. During the same period the population of Ballynakill parish increased by 37 per cent, while the Killian population increased by 25 per cent. These figures must be viewed with some caution as the statistics gathered for the 1821 and 1831 censuses are regarded as less accurate than subsequent census reports. Nevertheless there is evidence of a rapid rise in population in the districts concerned. This population increase resulted in a greater demand for land, resulting in higher rents, as well as subletting. Thus the problems identified in the evidence presented to the Devon Commission in 1844 would have been, in the absence of a resident landlord, endemic on the Netterville estate. With regard to the quality of housing, the 1841 census reported that the parish of Ballynakill had 262 fourth class houses out of a total of 295. Killian had 626 fourth class houses out of a total of 937 inhabited houses. Houses were graded from 1st class to 4th class, the latter being the poorest quality houses. This gives further indication that a majority of the inhabitants of both parishes were living at a bare subsistence level, as was typical of conditions in the west of Ireland generally at the time. In this regard Woodham Smith observes: 'In parts of the west of Ireland, more than three-fifths of the houses were one-roomed, windowless mud cabins, and west of a line from Londonderry to Cork, the proportion was two-fifths.'[16] Another negative factor was that the Netterville landlords had not lived on their estate since at least the mid-18th century. Consequently, the 'big house' and its attached employment opportunities were denied to the tenants on the estate, who in a completely rural location, had few other sources of paid employment. The increasing population created a demand for a limited supply of land. High rents, subdivision of land units and 'conacre' letting resulted. This meant that in poorer, densely populated areas, tenants rented land in return for their labour and the right to build a small cabin on a small plot, which would also provide potatoes as a staple food. 'Labourer and cottier shared a potato diet, with buttermilk as a luxury in good times.'[17] The end of the Napoleonic wars in 1815 drastically reduced the demand for grain and initiated a return to the raising of cattle, which was less labour-intensive. This presented the landowners with a problem. Their lands were now overpopulated with tenants. Those who could afford to be patient waited until leases ran out while others devised more pro-active methods of land clearance.

One of these strategies was the provision of assisted passage to other countries, particularly the United States and Canada. This strategy was, at different times, utilized by government, individual landlords and later by Poor Law Unions. An example of this occurred on the estate of Colonel Wandesforde, in Kilkenny, who by 1846 'had sent out 3,000 persons from Castlecomer at a cost of £5 each'.[18] Likewise, Lord Lansdowne spent £14,000 in clearing his Kerry estates in 1851. A news report in the *Nenagh Guardian* in 1846 noted '26 families, 146 persons sent out by Col. Wyndham from his estates near Limerick in the *Bryan Abbs* were paid the sum of £156 10s.'[19] Col. Wyndham held a large estate in Co. Clare and had been involved in assisted emigration from 1839 and was lauded by another newspaper for his transportation of tenants to the colonies, 'and securing there a competence and settlement for the poor cottiers who could not be accommodated on his estates'.[20] The article went on to state that a grant of 15s. a head was given on arrival in Canada. Sir Robert Gore Booth of Lissadell estate in County Sligo was also involved in assisted emigration programmes before and during the Famine. He chose to involve himself on a personal level in the arrangements, including involvement in selection of the *émigrés*, and 'took a great interest in the emigrants' welfare from the moment they left the property up to their arrival in North America'.[21] A near neighbour of John and Marcella Gerrard also displayed an interest in assisted emigration. Denis H. Kelly held substantial lands at Ballygar, Co. Galway, and informed the board of guardians at Ballinasloe workhouse in 1850 that he was 'willing to pay £10 for three inmates (presumably his former tenants) to help them emigrate to New Orleans'.[22] The board duly accepted his offer, resolved to give £10 more for that purpose and charged it to the Kileroran electoral division, where most of his estate was located.

Removal of tenants by this method allowed the landlord to reorganize the estate into larger holdings, put an end to the rundale system, remove the tenants from being a burden on the taxpayer, and possibly remove tenants who might be likely to become involved in agrarian protest. However, landlord-assisted emigration was patchy, though successful in estates where it was practised. It also helped to instigate publicly-funded assisted emigration, persuading some poor law unions to 'borrow on the rates to finance emigration passages, and thousands of workhouse residents emigrated to British colonies from 1840'.[23] Seasonal migration was quite commonplace along the western seaboard, where men would go to England and Scotland to earn money as farm labourers during the summer and harvest months, after which they would return to spend the winter at home. However, the onset of famine precipitated the mass of permanent emigration.

The Irish agricultural economy of the early 19th century was mainly tillage based, with potatoes and oats providing as much as 40 per cent of total agricultural output, compared to 11 per cent for cattle, butter and milk combined.[24] Despite poor quality soil in much of the country and the indifference of some absentee or spendthrift landlords, the agricultural economy succeeded in feeding a population which had risen by 3.5 million in 50 years. It also managed to produce a thriving export business. Nevertheless, it must be accepted that agricultural practices, compared to those of most of Britain, were backward, constrained as they were by the use of manual labour 'because draught animals and heavy ploughs were luxuries not suited to small farms, small fields and soils that were often wet or rocky.'[25] Perhaps another barrier to progress was the innate conservatism of the tenants. In this regard Coulter observed in 1862: 'The Irish peasant, or small farmer, is proverbial for his obstinate attachment to his old habits, and scarcely any amount of argument or persuasion will induce him to break through the thralldom of custom, or venture on the path of improvement.'[26]

The fact that many landlords were absentees also limited agricultural production, as, in the main, these absentee landlords were content to collect their rent without any thought for reinvestment, improvement, or land reclamation. Individual tenants however did reclaim patches of land, particularly for the growing of potatoes so that better land could be used for cereals. The main beneficiaries from agricultural output were the landlords and those who sublet land, 'while labourers and smallholders who paid the rents and were relatively heavy consumers of food, were the losers.'[27] The rising population and demand for land became a cause for concern for the parliament at Westminster resulting in the establishment of a parliamentary commission to enquire into the state of law and practice regarding the occupation of land in Ireland. The Devon Commission, so named because its chairman was William Courtney, earl of Devon, visited every part of Ireland and heard evidence from in excess of 1,000 witnesses. It heard evidence in Ballinasloe, Galway and Tuam and consequently gives a picture of the state of landholding in the vicinity of the district of the Netterville estate. While John Gerrard, husband of Marcella Netterville, did not give evidence to the commission, several of his neighbouring east Galway landlords did. Their evidence provided a picture of life and land use in the area at the time and offers persuasive evidence on the likely situation on the Netterville/Gerrard estate. James Clapperton, an agriculturalist, employed by Lord Clancarty of Garbally Park, Ballinasloe, described the land type in the area noting 'Rich, deep, heavy loams high in the scale of fertility are to be found in almost every locality; but this is only the exception. Peaty and moor soils are plentiful, and bog or turbary abundant.'[28] Witnesses generally were in agreement that where the landlord was resident conditions and farming practices were better. Another witness, referring to absentee landlords, observed that land agents whose task was to collect rents often sublet the task to under agents 'who are said to oppress the tenants very much'.[29] This 'oppression' was said to include the demand of payment for any type of favour received.

The practice of middlemen leasing large tracts of land from landlords and subletting it in smaller plots to under-tenants was also considered. This was deemed to be common and a barrier to improvement. It was suggested that the under-tenants often sublet again if prevailed upon to do so by a relative who was turned adrift from another holding. Thus the parcels of land became successively smaller and the population continued to rise. Another grievance raised in the evidence was that there was little incentive to improve land as the leases were short or nonexistent. The Ulster system, that is, the sale of tenant rights from one tenant to another, did not prevail, thus the tenant was not rewarded for carrying out improvements on land. Another witness to the commission was Denis H. Kelly, a landlord from Ballygar in east Galway, part of whose lands were adjacent to some of the Gerrard property. His evidence was consistent with that of other witnesses in the west, commenting on the extent of boggy soil in the district. He reported that, where possible, he put an end to the rundale system replacing it with divided farms. He noted that tillage farms were generally six to ten acres, and observed that there were a 'vast number of others which are a great deal too small; but we consider the tenants more in the light of cottiers or labourers, and not so much as able to make the rent out of the land.'[30] He went on to outline the provision he made for the paupers for which he could not make room.

> I set aside a proportion which they called Ballybeggarman; and instead of throwing them upon the roadside, I sacrificed a few acres and let them go there; and many of them have since emigrated to America or got holdings elsewhere; and those who have remained on it, have some of them become nailors [sic] and tradesmen and are earning rather a decent livelihood.[31]

It should be noted that the commission, in the main, heard evidence from landlords or large farmers. Nevertheless John Donnellan who farmed 50 acres in the barony of Athlone explained his plight. He held the land from an absentee landlord whom he had never seen and complained that he had 'expended upwards of £100 in building a house and he has served me notice to quit, and I cannot get a halfpenny for what I have expended if he turns me out.'[32] It appears that Mr Donnellan's father had taken the land on the promise of a lease from the land agent, a lease which never materialized. This suggests that there was some truth in the general perception that the estates of resident landlords were better managed. The bulk of evidence given to the commission in east Galway confirms a picture of growing demand for the available supply of land, and a consequent rise in the cost of renting land at a time when the export market for agricultural produce was in decline.

The available information on the Netterville family of Glasnevin and Longford, who held what became the Gerrard estate in the early 19th century, is somewhat sparse. The Glasnevin baptism records suggest that after his father's death, Frederick Netterville returned to Dublin. In any event he died a short few years afterwards in 1785 and was succeeded by Edmond, his eldest son, who died unmarried in 1814. In fact all three of Frederick's sons died young and unmarried – Frederick in Jamaica in 1807 and Robert in 1814. Shortly after her husband's death, his widow, Mary Keogh, remarried. Her second husband was Elias Corbally of Corbalton Hall near Tara in Co. Meath. It was here that Mary Keogh Netterville, accompanied by her three daughters, took up residence about the year 1790. Elias Corbally and Mary Keogh Netterville had two children of their own, Matthew and Louisa Corbally. Marcella Netterville's two full sisters Maria and Cressy died in 1823 and 1824 leaving Marcella Netterville as the beneficial owner of thousands of acres of land in east Galway. It is impossible to say if the will of Edmond Netterville of Longford was misplaced or ignored. The terms of the codicil clearly excluded Frederick and his children from inheriting the property, yet Marcella's accession to it seems to have been unchallenged, and remained so until after her death when a number of claimants emerged. In 1822, Marcella Netterville, then approximately 45 years of age, married John Gerrard of Gibbstown House near Navan, who subsequently adopted the name John Netterville Gerrard. At the time of the marriage, he was also in his mid-40s, and a substantial farmer. Griffith's Valuation of the mid-1850s shows him as the owner of a house, offices and land to the extent of 1,043 acres, with a valuation of £1,250, at Gibbstown Demesne in the parish of Donoughpatrick, barony of Kells Upper.[33] There were two herds' houses on the demesne as well as eight tenants who each occupied a house and garden at a valuation of 5s. annually. The lands were adjacent to the river Blackwater, a crucial factor for grazing land.

Arthur Young's *Tour of Ireland* describes a visit to a Mr Gerrard's farm at Gibbstown in June of 1776, describing it as 'one of the most considerable farms in the country.'[34] It is likely that the farm belonged to Samuel Gerrard, the father of John Gerrard, who would have been three years of age at the time. The account goes on to describe Mr Gerrard's practice of buying bullocks in October and selling them in summer with £4 profit. The report further notes that 'all the dry lands would do very well for turneps [sic]; Mr Ger[r]ard tried them and got fine crops: but the poor stole them in car loads which made him leave off the practice.'[35] Mr Gerrard also expressed the view that the best cattle came from Galway, Mayo and Roscommon and also referred to a nearby farm of 1,100 acres being let to sub-tenants and which 'does not produce a tythe [sic] of what it ought to do'.[36] The account shows that the Gibbstown lands were in the hands of the Gerrard family at the time, and also offers an insight into the family's approach to land management. The letting of land to tenants was frowned upon, and the brief flirtation with tillage in the form of turnips, probably as supplementary winter fodder, was abandoned because of pilfering. We are left with a picture of a substantial landowner who firmly believed in farming his own land and who was in the practice of travelling to fairs and markets in the counties of Galway, Roscommon and Mayo, buying store cattle in October for fattening on the rich grasslands of Meath for export or slaughter the following summer. Through his marriage to Marcella Netterville,

John Gerrard acquired some 7,000 acres in Galway. This gave him the opportunity to extend his very successful grazing empire to his newly acquired estate. From the perspective of the Galway tenants a landlord had been replaced by a farmer, whose mission was to actively farm the land. The world of the Meath grazier in the 19th century has been explored by Jim Gilligan, who examines the *modus operandi* of Edward Delaney, who farmed two holdings totalling 292 acres at Woodtown, in the vicinity of Dunshaughlin.

> He began stocking each year with a visit to the huge Ballinasloe fair in early October. He generally bought thirty cattle there and between the following March and May added up to eighty more. These were fattened during the summer and autumn and sold before the end of the year to be replaced by another set commencing in October ... He also traded in sheep using the visit to Ballinasloe in October to buy up to 100 wethers which were sold the following May and June at profits which rarely amounted to more than £1 per head. In June just before the wethers were sold, he bought in fifty hoggets on average which he fattened and sold off gradually from July to December, the sale of wool helping to boost his profits.[37]

John Gerrard's holdings at Gibbstown were considerably larger than Delaney's, and consequently his livestock figures would have been proportionately larger. His marriage to Marcella Netterville gave him access to substantial landholdings in Galway which had the potential to complement his main enterprise in Meath by providing a supply of livestock from the less fertile Galway lands for fattening on the plains of Meath. His task then as he saw it was to convert much of his wife's land to grazing pasture and the existence of a large number of tenants on the estate presented a barrier to its execution.

2. 'Awful extermination of tenantry'

The census of 1841 recorded the population of the country at 8,175,124. Given the rapid rate of increase of the previous 25 years, it is possible that the population of Ireland in 1846 may have been close to nine million people. Furthermore, this astonishing increase in population took place in the absence of any significant industrial development, thus placing additional pressure on the land. This pressure manifested itself in the form of increased cost of land rental, further subdivision of tiny farms and the subletting of land at even higher rates. In this regard, T.W. Freeman observes: 'there was undoubted pressure on the land, reflected in widespread poverty, strong competition for any available land, and a mass of labour unemployed for several months of the year.'[1]

Political decisions inadvertently contributed to the prevalence of small farms and the accompanying large population. An electoral law of 1793, which gave the vote to the occupiers or owners of holdings valued 40s. or more, provided an incentive for landlords to let holdings of a size less than 40s. valuation in order to limit the number of voters and thus protect the political *status quo*. This situation continued until 1829 when the figure was raised to £10. By this time the practice of subdivision into smaller farms had gained a momentum of its own. Seasonal emigration was one of the methods used to supplement family income. Men who went as farm labourers to England could expect to come home with £2–£3 if they went for the harvest and between £4 and £5 if they went for the full season.[2]

The 1841 census also gives valuable information about population density and farm size. The average number of persons per square mile of arable (or improved) land was 335 for the country as a whole and 386 in the province of Connacht. The 1841 population figures for the parish of Ballynakill show that the population was 1,559 on the 5,141 statute acres. This converts into a relatively modest 184 people per square mile. However the population of the townland of Ballinlass was 363, living on 572 statute acres of which some 50 acres was bogland and, according to the landlord, free of rent. Allowing for this gives a population density of 406 people per square mile, well above the provincial average, indicating that the townland was very densely populated and suffering from all the deprivation that accompanied such population density.[3]

It is difficult to pinpoint when exactly John Netterville Gerrard began to take an active part in the management of the estate following his marriage in

1822. It can be assumed that it took some years for him to become acquainted with the extent, usage and quality of the land in question. It is unlikely that his bride would have been of much help, given that she never lived on her estate and possibly rarely, if ever, visited the property prior to her marriage. The marriage settlement of John Gerrard and Marcella Netterville records the townlands that comprised the Galway estate, noting that they 'were then in the actual possession of the said Arthur James, Lord Killeen, and Mungo Henry Waller'[4], suggesting that the administration of the estate was overseen by Lord Kileen, Marcella Gerrard's brother-in-law. The first indication of the involvement of John Gerrard in the management of his Galway estates was in the year 1827 when he had his first encounter with his Ballinlass tenants. While he described it as a new proposal for tenancy, other accounts indicate that at least some of the Ballinlass tenants had been on the land for a considerable time as is evidenced by the response of Thady Rock in 1846 when he stated that he had lived in a particular house for nearly 70 years. The leasing of land to groups or 'companies' of tenants was widespread in the locality before the Famine. Each company would appoint a 'head man', who dealt with the landlord and then allocated the land among the members of the company. Additionally, the practice of so-called 'middlemen' renting substantial portions of land from landlords was also prevalent. The middleman leased the land from the landlord at an agreed rate and then sublet some or all of the land to under-tenants at a higher rate per acre. This created a situation where a landlord had tenants on his land who were not directly accountable to him, and with whom he had little or no interaction. John Gerrard later described his land at Ballinlass as comprising 300 acres, Irish plantation measure, including some 50 acres of bogland. The first edition of the Ordnance Survey map shows the townland as 572 statute acres. He outlined the terms and conditions of the lease:

> In the year 1827 thirty persons sent me a proposal in writing to become my tenants, at a rent of £1 10s. an acre for the upland (nothing for the bog). I kept that proposal, allowed those thirty into possession under it and received from one (the principal of them) the rent half yearly up to the 1st of March 1842.[5]

It is possible that in 1827, the lease held by the Ballinlass tenants was about to expire, and their proposal was to renew an existing lease. This might explain an apparent contradiction between John Gerrard's account and Thady Rock's claim that he had lived in Ballinlass for nearly 70 years. John Gerrard's assertion that he received all of the rent from one person is also significant, in that he had delegated the collection of the individual rents to the head tenant. He outlined the difficulties which arose in his relationship with the tenants.

In the period intervening between the 1827 and the 1st of March 1842, those tenants sublet considerable portions of the land to about forty miserable persons, from whom they extracted, in some instances, a rent of £2, £2 10s. and even £3 per acre. I did everything I could at all times, by remonstrances, to prevent the subletting: and to stop if possible. I insisted on the full rent being paid by the principal of the thirty tenants, and never in any instance recognised or received rent from the under tenants.[6]

This suggests that the root cause of the evictions at Ballinlass was a dispute about subletting and the landlord's refusal to have any dealings with under-tenants. The matter only arose when there was a problem with the payment of rent, suggesting that the landlord initially was prepared to tolerate subletting as long as the rent was paid. However a statement by the lawyer engaged by the Ballinlass tenants to defend the ejectment offers a different perspective to the situation. Some time after the evictions, the resident magistrate interviewed the lawyer, Henry O'Loughlin, who stated that while Mr Gerrard's account was mainly correct, some facts were suppressed by him. Mr O'Loughlin went on to state:

Previous to the year 1827, the lands of Ballinlass were occupied by about 70 families, and the greatest poverty prevailed amongst them, Mr Gerrard, not wishing to have so many paupers on his estate and anxious to get rid of them, did let, that year, the lands of Ballinlass to thirty families upon the offered conditions that these thirty tenants were to banish off the lands the other 40 families, upon a penalty of £5 per acre for failing to do so.[7]

This statement implies that John Gerrard knew full well of the situation regarding over-population and subletting, and expected the 30 tenants to carry out a clearance on his behalf. It may also explain why he granted no formal lease. It is likely that his experiences with his Ballinlass tenants hardened John Gerrard's attitude towards letting in general and increased his resolve to turn his Galway estate into grazing land to complement his estate at Gibbstown. He also indicated that his dispute with his Ballinlass tenants was not his sole dispute with tenants on the Netterville estate. He described the circumstances which led to his eviction of tenants from the townland of Newbridge, saying:

It was held under a very old lease for three lives: and on the death of the surviving life the tenants, instead of settling with me for a new tenancy, as I was desirous they should do, thought proper to allege that the last old life was not dead, and they set up the life of a person of the

same name as that last life, although not born for several years after the
execution of the lease.[8]

The statement indicates that he was willing to renew the lease. However,
it raises a question as to why the tenants, fearing that he would not, resorted
to duplicitous behaviour. John Gerrard then described the tenants' defence of
his ejectment, noting that the tenants 'actually employed an attorney who took
defence to my ejectment'.[9] He observed that for this he was 'designated a cruel
landlord for turning out such fraudulent people.'[10] It is likely that the eviction
of tenants at Newbridge took place about the year 1841. A notice from a
shopkeeper named Michael O'Connor was published in *The Nation* in January
1843. O'Connor stated that he had successfully kept an 'assorted establishment'
in Newbridge, lately called Newtown Gerrard, for 16 years. He went on to
assert that he had always paid his way and was willing to pay 'a trifle of rent
due to his landlord John N. Gerrard Esq.'[11] It was about 1840–1 that the village
of Newtown Gerrard was constructed, and John Gerrard may have been intent
on removing any merchant who would provide competition to his new
enterprise. In the first report from Ballinlass dated 25 March 1846, Redmond,
a reporter from the *Freeman's Journal*, described his approach to the Gerrard
estate. He wrote of a place having once been known as Newbridge, but latterly
called Newtown Gerrard. John and Marcella Gerrard attempted to create a
new settlement there by building a market house, inn and constabulary
barracks. The venture was an abject failure. The barracks was never occupied,
despite the strenuous efforts of the Gerrards, and the market house was not
utilized, possibly because it was boycotted by the tenants. The report described
the market house as 'without merchandise, neither buyer or seller appearing
there, and the rusty iron triangle, with mouldering beam and scales attached,
speak eloquently of the neglected state of this deserted village.'[12] The first
edition of the six inch Ordnance Survey map published in 1838 shows no
evidence of such a settlement, indicating that it was built later than 1837 when
the area was surveyed. It is likely that John Gerrard viewed Michael O'Connor
as a business rival and contrived to remove him and the other tenants for purely
business reasons. During this period, Newtown Gerrard also became a location
for regular fairs. Provincial newspapers such as the *Tuam Herald* and the *Nenagh
Guardian* included Newtown Gerrard in its list of fairs and markets in the years
1841–83.

His encounter with the Newbridge tenants, coupled with the failure of his
estate town, may have been the last straw for John Gerrard, who probably
inherited an antipathy towards tenants from his father. In 1842 the matter of
subletting in Ballinlass came to a head. He stated that when the September
rent of 1842 was demanded in the usual way from the original 30 tenants, 'they
one and all refused to pay it, alleging that they would only pay the rents of

January 30, 1843.

MICHAEL O'CONNOR, of Newbridge, lately
called Newtown Gerrard, in the Parish and Barony of
Killyan, and County of Galway, who kept an assorted Establishment in said town for the last sixteen years, traded in
England and Ireland to the amount of 72,000l. and upwards,
and now challenges all whom he ever had a dealing with to
be able to call to him for one penny ; that without closing,
compounding, or compromising, but paying 20s. to every pound
sterling, with the exception of a trifle of rent due to his landlord, John N. Gerrard, Esq., Gibbstown, County Meath,
which he is ready to pay when called for. Also, he having
been entrusted with surveys of Conacres and Personal Properties since he took his diploma from Dublin Castle to the
amount at least of 100,000l., and now stands without cen-
sure ; and always paid the greatest attention to do justice be-
ween Landlord and Tenant.
             I am, &c. &c.,
                         MICHAEL O'CONNOR.

2 Statement from Michael O'Connor.

the portion of land under their own actual occupation; and their under-tenants
were unable to pay any rent, that I should settle with those under-tenants as
best I could.'[13] He added that the same answer was given to the rent demand
in March and September 1843 and March 1844. He began ejectment
proceedings in the Easter term of 1844. The ejectment was vigorously opposed
by the tenants at the summer assizes in Galway in 1844. The tenants' main
defence was that John Gerrard did not actually sign the proposal of 1827.
However the Galway jury found in his favour declaring that there was a sum
of £708 9s. 10d. due to him in rent arrears.

The eviction of tenants in the townland of Ballinlass took place on Friday
13 March 1846. The evictions, although witnessed by a large crowd of people,
were carried out without any breach of the peace, possibly due to the presence
of policemen and soldiers. On the morning in question, the sheriff,
accompanied by a large force of the 49th Regiment under the command of
Captain Browne and a detachment of police led by Sub-Inspector Cummins,
arrived at Ballinlass and 'proceeded to the place marked out for destruction'.[14]
The people were then called upon to render possession, 'and forthwith the
bailiffs of Mrs Gerrard commenced the work of demolition'.[15] The roofs and
portion of the walls were demolished. Houses were demolished during
evictions to ensure that they were not reoccupied by the former tenants or
taken over by squatters. This adds further weight to the view that the purpose
of the eviction was to clear the land for grazing purposes, and that there was
no question of a last-minute reprieve for those who offered to pay the rent.

A man and a woman who had fever were carried from their own house into another after possession had been taken of it, and they were permitted to remain there. This was the only house left standing. The evictions were reported in the *Roscommon Journal* on the following day, 14 March 1846. The brief report entitled 'Awful extermination of tenantry', gave the number of evicted persons at 447 and incorrectly reported that a child had been killed by a falling beam. The final sentence of the report stated 'If we are correctly informed, Mr and Mrs Gerrard have dispossessed upwards of two thousand human beings within the last few years.'[16] This story, in the course of the next few weeks, was picked up by other newspapers including the *Freeman's Journal,* which dispatched a reporter, Mr S. Redmond, to the scene. Redmond arrived in Ballinlass on Wednesday, 25 March, almost two weeks after the evictions, accompanied by Mr Donovan, a shopkeeper and resident of Ballygar, a small market town some eight miles distant. Redmond submitted his reports to his newspaper in the form of seven letters dated Wednesday 25 to Tuesday 31 March. Redmond subsequently published these letters in pamphlet form. The reporter described his arrival in Ballinlass 'along a kind of a road or *togher* as it is called'[17] and noticed some dung (i.e., farmyard manure) on the roadside. This had been dumped there by some of the evicted tenants in order to prevent it becoming the property of the landlord following the eviction. The settlement was described as consisting of 67 houses, and all but one having been completely destroyed. The wrecked houses showed evidence of being 'comfortable, clean and neat kept habitations, with snug kitchen gardens either before or behind them'.[18] Scattered among the ruins were items of broken crockery, household furniture, cooking utensils and farming implements. Eyewitnesses told the reporter that on the night of the eviction, some of the evicted tenants erected some crude shelters against the remaining walls of the cottages. On the following day the bailiffs returned and completely destroyed the remains of the cottages, including the foundations. As the reporter began to speak with some of the evictees, he discovered that many of the older generation could only converse in Irish, as he observed:

> although I have often regretted that I was ignorant of the Irish language, I never really felt the want of it until yesterday; and, although I could not understand it, yet it drew tears from my eyes to hear the energy and earnestness with which the poor creatures spoke in the expressive language of their native land.[19]

Redmond used the services of his companion Mr Donovan as an interpreter. The reporter then met an old man, who was evicted from his home and questioned him as follows,

Are you one of the people who were recently turned out? I enquired.
Indeed I am Sir, said he with a heavy sigh.
How old are you, Sir?
Nearly eighty.
How long did you reside in the village of Ballinlass?
Over sixty-eight years, Sir, said he, and burst into tears.
How many in family have you?
Three, together with myself, but I had a great deal more than that. Some
of them are dead and gone, and well for them that they didn't live to
see this desolate day; others of them are married and some are gone to
America.
How much land had you?
Why, I can't rightly tell, as there were no regular farms, but there was
over 400 acres belonging to the village.
Did you owe any rent?
I did, sir.
Were you able to pay it?
I was, sir, and willing to, but she wouldn't take it for the last five years.
Why so?
Why, because sir, she wanted to throw down the house to make bullock
pastures.
Did you ever offer the rent to the lady?
I did, Sir, more than twenty times, and offered it to her agent also, but
they would not take it. We went to the hall-door often with the rent,
but they wouldn't take it off us. Every man in the village but one offered
the rent over and over, but they wouldn't take it, and we offered to pay
the man's rent, but they wouldn't take that either.[20]

The man, Thady Rock, went on to confirm that the bailiffs prevented the
evictees sheltering in the ruins the night after the eviction, and that roadside
fires were also put out. Thady Rock's answer to the question regarding the
extent of his landholding merits some examination. His reply was that he did
not rightly know, as there were no regular farms but that there were over 400
acres belonging to the village. The reply indicates that the lands were farmed
on the lines of the 'village' or rundale system as described in a pamphlet on
the system operated on the lands of Lord Clonbrock at Ahascragh some
10 miles distant.

> At first perhaps one family rented a large tract of land: but in process of
> time, as a son or daughter married, an out-house, or cow-cabin became
> the residence of the new married couple and a portion of ground was
> assigned to them. Thus the holdings (or small tenements) became

subdivided, not with permanent fences, so as to ensure to each person his own plot; but according to the variable regulations made by the heads of the village. The tillage land of one person this year, being allotted to another next year, whilst the grazing land was regulated by so many head of cattle to each portion called collips: such sub-divisions have been carried on, till the claims of the family have been a fortieth or fiftieth part of the whole.[21]

The existence of this village system is confirmed by the 1838 Ordnance Survey map which shows Crow Village and Tansy's Village in the adjacent townland of Cloonavihony as well as Doyle's Village and Dunn's Village in the nearby townland of Rushestown. The brief report submitted by Sub-inspector Cummins to Dublin Castle noted: 'Eighty houses were levelled to the ground and no resistance offered by the people, several of whom had cleared off previous to our going there.'[22] The report went on to state: 'The tenants and labourers of Mr Gerrard from another part of his property were obliged to attend there (very much against their will) in order to assist in levelling those houses by the directions of a Mr Holmes and the steward who attended there for Mr Gerrard.'[23] These reports clearly indicate that there was no question of tenants being allowed to remain in their homes as caretakers, further suggesting that the real purpose of the evictions was land clearance for the creation of grazing farms.

On the following day the reporter visited Mount Bellew and spoke with more of the evictees in the presence of Mr Dennehy, the head constable at Mount Bellew. The head constable confirmed that he had witnessed the evictions and had been most distressed by the cries and screams of the women and children as they clung to the door posts 'from whence they were dragged by the bailiffs'.[24] Mr Dennehy also indicated that the settlement at Ballinlass was a peaceful and law-abiding community and 'there never was a breach of the peace or any other charge made against them.'[25] The constable also indicated that in the previous three-and-a-half years, Mrs Gerrard had turned out more than 4,000 people. While this figure may not be totally accurate, it is a further indication that the evictions at Ballinlass were more than an isolated dispute about rent arrears and subletting, and that a change from tillage to grazing was the real purpose of the Ballinlass evictions, and was part of a concerted effort by Gerrard to clear his estate of tenants. Similarly, the eviction of tenants at Newbridge about the year 1842 was more than a dispute about a lease. The fundamental question of rent payment in Ballinlass remained unresolved. Several of the tenants attested that they had offered the rent but that it was refused. John Gerrard, however, indicated that the tenants from 1842 offered the rent of the land actually under their occupation, and when legal proceedings began, ceased to pay rent at all. An interesting exchange took place on Friday, 27 March, when the reporter paid another visit to Ballinlass. He spoke to Thady Kilmartin and his family, Matthew Rock and also to Paddy Kenny, who was one of the bailiffs at the eviction.

> *When did you offer to pay the rent?*
> I offered it every May and November for the last five half years.
> *Did the other tenants offer the rent also?*
> Every one of them but one sir!
> *The herd, Kenny, here says you neither paid rent, nor offered to pay it; is that true?*
> No sir, it is not, and I say before his face, we did offer to the rent, every May and November.
> *Is that true Kenny?*
> I don't know.
> You know it is, and I say we did offer to pay it.
> Sure if you did, you would not have been ejected. (Kenny)
> Don't you know in your heart and soul, said Rock, that we offered the rent and it would not be taken.
> Didn't Mr Holmes (the head agent and attorney of Mrs Gerrard, as I was informed) come down here last harvest along with Mr O'Loughlin (the gentleman who acted as law agent for the poor people) and wasn't your crop going to be seized for the rent, and didn't you then, to save the crop, make an agreement with the gentlemen, and sign your hands to it?
> Yes, we signed a paper, but did not know what it was about, as we left it all to our attorney, but they turned it against us.[26]

These exchanges may hold the key to the dispute. Both Thady and Matthew Rock said that all of the tenants but one had offered the rent and it had been refused. Further enquiries by the reporter indicated that the one tenant in question may have been the head tenant, the only tenant that the landlord had dealt with directly. He was named as Tom Gavin who had rented land to the value of £80 and was, in fact, a middleman rather than a farmer. He had taken in a number of under-tenants who by 1842 were unable to pay their rents which were apparently as high as £2. 10s. per acre. To complicate matters further the bailiff, Paddy Kenny, stated that when the original 30 tenants rented the lands in 1827, there were undertenants already on the land and 'the thirty tenants who took the land altogether at 30s. an acre about 17 years ago, let the undertenants remain.'[27] This goes some way in explaining how the number of original tenants was 30, whereas the number of households actually evicted was more than 60. The report continued with the statement,

Gavin went away to another part of the country where his daughter had got married. He left his land at Ballinlass to the people and told them to do what they liked with it. It was alleged that he owed £40 and until this was paid, no rent would be taken from the tenants except 'on account' and as they owed nothing they refused to take receipts 'on account'.[28]

Thady Rock had also asserted that the remaining tenants had also offered to pay Tom Gavin's rent. If this were the case, the only item at issue was the arrears of £40 owed by Tom Gavin. Given that the matter of subletting had occurred from the very outset of the lease, it is difficult to escape the conclusion that the dispute was little more than a pretext to clear the land for grazing purposes, thus continuing the process which seems to have begun in Newbridge in 1841. Paddy Kenny's reference to the crops being seized for the rent was also referred to in John Gerrard's response to the negative publicity engendered by the evictions. His rebuttal was published In *Saunder's News Letter*, a pro-landlord Dublin newspaper, on 3 April 1846, and subsequently published in many newspapers in Ireland and Great Britain, including the *Roscommon Journal*, on 4 April 1846. It seems that the signed agreement referred to by Paddy Kenny was an agreement to vacate the lands in order to save the crops then in the ground. This was subsequently confirmed by John Gerrard who stated that as a final attempt to settle the dispute, he sent

> A professional gentleman from Dublin to have an interview with the defendants, and to propose to them on my behalf that they should be forgiven the large arrears of rent and the costs then due – be allowed to take the crops then in ground free of all rents, which crops at the time valued at £700 or £800 – and be allowed to remain in undisturbed possession of their homes and lands until the 1st of February 1846.[29]

Thady Rock's response that the tenants did not know what they were signing may be correct, as it is unlikely that all of the tenants were literate, and many were unfamiliar with the English language. Furthermore, it must be remembered that they were relatively new to tenant matters as their head tenant had carried out all business from 1827 until 1842. On the other hand it is entirely possible that they knew full well what they had agreed to, as a desperate measure to save their crops, and lived in hope that something would turn up in the following six months. The reporter then asked Thady Rock where he then lived, and how he supported himself. Rock replied that he lived on Mr Cheevers' property, (a neighbouring resident landlord), but that he had no means of supporting his family of eight persons apart from 'not eight baskets of potatoes'[30] which would last less than a fortnight. 'God help me, I don't know what to do or where to go'[31] was his tearful response to a question as to how he might live in the future.

On the following day while the reporter was at the market in Ballygar some eight miles distant a woman who was known to be a widow approached him. She told him that she was a tenant of Mr Gerrard in Crow Village, in the townland of Cloonavihony, which is adjacent to Ballinlass. She had been served with an eviction notice which she showed to the reporter. The eviction notice, dated 13 March 1846, was against Celia Connor and Mary Mahon, otherwise Carr. Several other inhabitants of this village were present and were in similar circumstances. Redmond seemed satisfied with the authenticity of the document as he quoted it in full in his article.[32]

In his final report from the area, the reporter wrote about a meeting with three Roman Catholic clergymen at the bridge of Newtown Gerrard (Newbridge), two miles from Ballinlass. The clergymen gave information of events at Newtown Gerrard in 1841. They claimed that there had been a thriving settlement there until a tenant shopkeeper named Connor had allegedly displeased Mrs Gerrard and she had him evicted, despite the fact that his father was ill and had to be 'carried out and laid on a bed on the road, and died three days after.'[33] This account appears to confirm the facts of the notice published by Michael O'Connor and was in marked difference to the account presented by John Gerrard in his article in the *Roscommon Journal*. Gerrard also stoutly defended the actions of his bailiffs during the eviction itself. He claimed that in the course of the eviction 'a number of persons in my employment attended for the purpose of assisting the people to remove, and take down their houses'.[34] He further claimed that on his instructions a doctor was called to attend on sick families who were allowed to remain in their houses and lands and who continued to remain there. This particular assertion seems to have been untrue as the reporter, Redmond, carried out a detailed inspection of the townland and found no sign of habitation. John Gerrard also indicated that from the due date of possession, 1 February 1846, he had made available men, horses and carts at his own expense 'to such of the persons as desired to move off the lands their provisions, manure and furniture of their houses and that some of the tenants had availed of this offer.'[35] He further contended that in the course of the eviction his men were very careful in taking down the houses so that very little of the timber was broken and that the dispossessed were permitted to take it away with them. He made the astonishing claim that his agent treated the evictees with such kindness that 'several of them at the time, and since, thanked him for so treating them'.[36] A more credible observation regarding evictions in general is offered in a recent work by L.P. Cutris. 'The awesome sight of heavily armed police and soldiers parading through the district and aiding and abetting the bailiffs in their callous work could hardly be forgotten by those who bore witness.'[37] John Gerrard also claimed to have given £4 each to the four widows who were among his 30

3. Local monument commemorating Ballinlass evictions.

original tenants. He vehemently denied anybody was injured and described the claim that a child was killed in a woman's arms as 'a falsehood'. He claimed that the amount of rent due to him as of 1 March 1846 was '£1,062 18s. besides poor rates, county rates, and the costs of the proceedings'.[38] The letter concluded with a contention by Mr Gerrard that he had carried on extensive works, given great employment, and posed the question 'is it not a very great hardship that I have been dragged before the public in the manner that I have been lately in relation to my estate in the county of Galway.'[39]

The available evidence suggests that John Gerrard's land clearances began as early as 1840, around the time he invested a considerable amount of capital in the construction of Newtown Gerrard. It is difficult to reconcile his vision of a busy village with its inn, constabulary barracks and busy market house with a depopulated district. On the other hand the building of a barracks in the expectation that it would be occupied by police perhaps suggests that he was expecting resistance to his planned clearances. It is also possible that he was attempting to emulate his neighbour Christopher Dillon Bellew of Mount Bellew, who had built the village of Newtown Bellew on his estate. It is clear that well before the Famine, John Gerrard was engaged in a systematic clearance of tenants off his lands and that the reason, as succinctly articulated by Thady Rock, was because he 'wanted to throw down the house to make bullock pastures.'[40]

3. An uncontrollable fancy for pasture

By 1846, evictions were relatively commonplace in many parts of Ireland. Many landlords were involved in various schemes of improving or 'striping' their lands, involving the removal or relocation of tenants, and were able to do so in the absence of any public outcry outside the immediate vicinity of their estates. In this context it is possible that John Gerrard was somewhat taken aback at the widespread publicity and public outcry that followed his actions at Ballinlass. The publicity generated by the evictions indicated the growing influence of newspapers, provincial and national, in the daily life of the country. The national school system was by then developing apace, and with it the teaching of English in the schools. In addition, with the growing level of emigration as a response to population growth, it was now clear that English language was a necessity for success in the new world. The existence of a canal system and a developing railway network contributed to a wider distribution of goods, including newspapers. The *clachan* housing system, which was so prevalent in pre-Famine Ireland, provided a ready audience for a newspaper story if there was even one person in the community who could read. Thus the Ireland of 1846 was ready for reports on evictions that gave the tenants' side of the story.

The *Freeman's Journal* account of the events at Ballinlass followed by John Gerrard's staunch defense of his actions caused much debate and comment in the newspapers of the time in Ireland and Great Britain. It is hardly surprising that the newspapers' political leanings dictated whether the comments were supportive of the Ballinlass tenantry or were sympathetic to the position of the landlord. For its own part, the *Freeman's Journal* printed Mr Gerrard's rebuttal in full on 2 April 1846. However in its editorial of the same issue it dismissed his defense with the observation that questions remained about the motives and origin of the ejectment, while acknowledging that 'Mr Gerrard acted with all legality, we admit; nay, we *complain* that all he did was strictly legal'.[1] The editorial concluded with a demand that the law be changed to prevent such ejectments. On the other hand the *Belfast News-Letter*, in an editorial entitled 'One story is good until another is told', accepted Mr Gerrard's statement in full, noting that 'the "commissioners" who had been dispatched by the Repeal newspapers to the scene of action, burdened the columns of their employers with the most fearful details of the misery said to be endured with its victims.'[2] The editorial observed that following the publication of Mr Gerrard's response 'the case is at once altered'. The editorial concluded: 'Such is the case out of which the factious Repeal press has elaborated a false and malicious charge against a kind and benevolent, but ill-used, landlord; and such we are convinced, is the true history of two-thirds of the "clearances" effected in Ireland.'[3] However an editorial in *The Times* was far less supportive of Mr Gerrard's letter, noting that his defense 'shows the sublime indifference to social considerations of which no one but an Irish landowner is capable.'[4] Some days later, the same newspaper published a letter from a correspondent, describing themselves as an onlooker, referred to the party of bailiffs as consisting of '12 carts, each having four men as levelers, and in each cart a supply of spades, pick-axes, and crow-bars, brought out with the military and police'.[5] The letter also asked if some of the tenants vacated their homes on the night before the evictions and 'erected a few sticks, with a blanket over them for shelter on the other side of the road, was not such torn down over them, and they driven off?'[6] On 3 April 1846, the *Belfast News-Letter* noted that Col. McGregor, at the instance of the government, had come to Mount Bellew to investigate the matter. It is likely that the investigating officer was none other than Duncan McGregor, inspector general of the Constabulary. In his report, Col. McGregor commented on the account furnished by Sub-inspector Cummins noting that it was 'perfectly correct and the numbers dispossessed by no means exaggerated ... in a state of misery not to be described, scattered over the neighbourhood, residing in the ditches or anywhere they can find shelter.'[7] The report also suggested that prior to the evictions; Mr Gerrard had been advised by some of his landlord neighbours that he give a sum of money to his Ballinlass tenants to facilitate their emigration to America. Mr Gerrard's reported response was that he would not give them a farthing.

A few weeks after the evictions, the parish priest of Mount Bellew, Fr Fitzpatrick, wrote to the *Freeman's Journal* reporting the death of one of the evictees. He named the deceased man as Lacky Rock and wrote that he and his family consisting of a wife and six children 'were obliged to seek shelter by the ditch side, where he caught the cold, which this day terminated in his death.'[8] The same newspaper contains another letter also reporting the death of an eviction victim named Loughlen Carrick. It is likely, given the bilingual nature of the district at the time, that this refers to the same person, Loughlen Carrick being an Irish version of Lacky Rock.

Given this level of publicity, it was perhaps inevitable that the matter arose in both houses of parliament. In the house of commons, William Smith O'Brien, member for the constituency of Limerick, sought an investigation to be carried out by 'the stipendiary magistrates and other officers of the Irish constabulary... and that such reports may be laid before parliament as early as possible.'[9] Prior to proposing this measure, Mr O'Brien read a long statement into the record of the house. The statement was, in fact, the full text of

Redmond's first letter from Ballinlass, which had been published in the *Freeman's Journal* on 27 March 1846 and which described the evictions and named all the evicted families. Given the political situation in Ireland it is not surprising that the matter was raised by O'Brien, who by this time had become disenchanted with the ageing Daniel O'Connell and was becoming increasingly sympathetic towards the more revolutionary Young Ireland movement. At the same time, Sir Robert Peel's government was in terminal decline in the aftermath of the repeal of the corn laws and presumably was in no mood for another Irish enquiry. The proposal received a lukewarm response from Sir James Graham, the home secretary, who noted that parliament had no information on the matter other than a newspaper report and 'that the House should suspend their judgment, these allegations having been met by a positive denial.' [10]

The evictions and resultant publicity were also raised in the house of lords on 30 April 1846. The marquis of Londonderry told the Lords that he was 'very much struck by reading the extraordinary statements which had appeared in the newspapers.' [11] The marquis of Clanrickard added that from his own enquiries he believed that the facts were as they had been represented: and that it appeared to him that there was 'a proper case for enquiring, and one illustrating the necessity for a change in the law of landlord and tenant.' [12] On 3 April 1846 an attempt to have John Gerrard's letter to *Saunder's News-Letter* read into the record of the Lords was unsuccessful. Lord Clancarty informed the Chamber that he had a copy of a letter addressed to the marquis of Londonderry, who was abroad and would be away for some time. The letter was from John G. Holmes, attorney to Mr Gerrard, and requested that the enclosed letter by Mr Gerrard to the newspaper be read to the Lords. However, Lord Clancarty stated that he considered the letter to be an *ex parte* situation and declined to read it. This may be indicative of Lord Clancarty's disapproval of John Gerrard's actions. The term *ex parte* implies that only one side of a dispute is being represented. This aspect seems to have troubled Lord Clancarty far more than it troubled Smith O'Brien, who had no such scruples about reading Redmond's first report into the record of the house of commons.

While the actual evictions at Ballinlass appear, according to reports, to have passed off peacefully, probably due to the large force of constabulary and troops, there is evidence of subsequent retaliation against the landlord. In May 1846 newspapers reported on the maiming of cattle on the estate. The *Nenagh Guardian* reported that 100 head of cattle were houghed on the Gerrard estate, [13] while on the previous day the *Freeman's Journal*, apparently reporting on the same incident, described it as the 'tailing' of eight animals. [14] The maiming of livestock was an integral part of agrarian protest at the time. The term 'houghing' was ascribed to the severing of tendons and ligaments of the hind legs of the animal thus rendering it immobile. Tailing was a milder form of disapproval. It involved the removal of all or part of the animal's tail, involving pain and blood loss, which would be followed by a full recovery. The disparity in the accounts suggests that the source of the information was based on rumour rather than fact. Nevertheless it is clear that there existed an atmosphere of smoldering resentment towards the landlord in question. In May of the following year the *Times* reported that a herd employed by Mrs Gerrard discovered a body, buried in a shallow grave at the townland of Clonkeen on the Gerrard property. It was found, upon examination, that the deceased had a large contusion on the left ear. Police were called and an inquest was told that the deceased had been strangled. The report, in suggesting the perpetrators were local, observed 'it is considered that none but those connected with the place would have so secretly and adroitly interred him in it.'[15] While there is no direct evidence linking this murder with the Gerrard clearances, it provides a further insight into the general atmosphere in the district at the time.

Despite the vast amount of publicity and approbation, there is no evidence that John Gerrard showed any remorse for his actions at Ballinlass. A brief report in *The Nation* in April 1847 probably added further to his tarnished reputation. The paper reported the death of a man named Gibbons on the roadside near Mount Bellew, a market town some two miles south of Ballinlass. The newspaper added that the death had occurred on Sunday evening and that the body was still on the roadside the following day, 'no coffin having been provided'. The report concluded with the information, 'He was one of the tenants ejected by Mrs Gerrard from Ballinlass'.[16] The list of evicted families, published in Redmond's first report from Ballinlass contained the name of Pat Gibbons, the sole member of a household. It is likely that he was the person whose death was reported. Some two weeks later Revd Patrick McLoughlin, a Catholic curate, reported on the number of famine deaths in the parish of Ballynakill, which included the townland of Ballinlass. He reported that during the period 31 October 1846 to 1 April 1847, there were 56 deaths in the parish, compared to 10 fatalities for the same period in the previous year. He added that 30 of the deaths were caused by starvation. The priest observed that some of those who died were strangers passing through the parish, whereas 'others who died were of the number of those poor people who were about this time last year ejected from the lands of Ballinlass.'[17] This report suggests that the fate of many of the Ballinlass evictees was destitution, starvation and death. Fr McLoughlin also commended the Mount Bellew landlord, Sir M.D. Bellew, Bart., for his provision of relief works for people 'no matter whose tenants they were.'[18] Despite these stark reminders of the consequences of his actions at Ballinlass there is evidence that John Gerrard's policy of land clearance, which began at Newbridge in 1841, continued unabated. In November 1848 the *Freeman's Journal* reported 'Fifteen families,

making in all sixty-seven people have just been evicted from the Connor
village, a portion of the Gerrard property.'[19] The report continued that the
evictees, some of whom were widows and orphans, were wandering about,
'begging, often in vain'. The report concluded by naming the householders
evicted as well as the number in each household. Neither the 1838 Ordnance
Survey six inch map, nor the subsequent Griffith's Valuation show a place
named Connor village on the Gerrard estate. However, a local historian, John
Joe Crehan, born in 1926, has suggested that the location of this clearance may
have been in the townland of Laghacrogher, near Newbridge, which was then
known as Newtown Gerrard.[20] The settlement at this location was known
locally as Corner village. The 1838 Ordnance Survey map shows a significant
settlement at this location, adjacent to a right-angled bend on the road.
Griffith's Valuation, published in the 1850s, indicates that the townland of
Laghacrogher, comprising 126 statute acres, was held 'in fee' by John N.
Gerrard. The census reports indicate that this townland had a population of
116 in 1841. This had fallen to five in 1851 and to zero by 1861.[21] This adds
some credence to the suggestion that this was the location of Connor or
Corner village.

What may have been John Gerrard's final clearance on his Galway estate
took place in the townland of Kilcoosh in September of 1853. He had
purchased the townland earlier that year under the Encumbered Estates Act.
The land had been owned by Geoffrey Davies, a distant relative of Marcella
Netterville-Gerrard. Davies was to reappear after the death of Marcella Gerrard
in 1865. Most of the tenants held a seven-year lease which began on 1
November 1847. However, the conditions of sale noted: 'This letting under
the Court, will expire on the sale, and the purchaser will be entitled to
immediate possession, subject to enablements.'[22] The townland consisted of
384 acres and contained 42 families, a total of 216 persons 'and when Mr
Gerrard made the purchase they offered to pay him their rent up to the first
instant but he would not permit them to remain as he wanted the land for his
own use.'[23] The first attempt at clearance took place in September, when the
sub-sheriff, accompanied by 11 constables, arrived at Kilcoosh and demanded
possession from the 42 families. There was no trouble, the tenants being
permitted to remain on their lands so that they could harvest their crops which
were still in the ground. The tenants, in turn, agreed to vacate by 1 November
1853. This did not happen, with the result that on 11 November the sub-sheriff
returned, this time accompanied by bailiffs and a force of 36 constables. When
the party arrived at Kilcoosh they were confronted by a group 'upwards of
400 men and women who evinced a determination of resistance.'[24] When the
bailiffs attempted to demolish some of the dwellings the crowd became even
more hostile and unruly with the result that the sub-sheriff deemed it prudent
to withdraw.

Table 3.1. Gerrard landholdings in Ballynakill and Killian parishes, 1854

Townland	Parish	Total Acres	Tenanted Acres	Total Valuation £
Ballinlass	Ballynakill	572	0	250
Carrownagappul	Ballynakill	1059	0	187
Longford	Ballynakill	335	0	170
Ballynacorra*	Killian	111	111	44
Ballynalaghy	Killian	258	23	60
Boherbannagh	Killian	299	46	77
Cloonavihony	Killian	453	105	118
Cloughbrack	Killian	65	65	19
Cloonkeen*	Killian	95	0	20
Gunnode	Killian	632	77	130
Kilcoosh	Killian	381	0	65
Laghacrogher	Killian	126	0	30
Newbridge	Killian	200	0	128
Newgrove	Killian	154	0.25	53
Newvillage	Killian	137	0	52
Rushestown	Killian	883	548	227
Summerhill	Killian	225	0	130
Toghergar	Killian	43	0	21
Toomard	Killian	254	242	41
Tully	Killian	106	0	28
Windfield	Killian	404	8	231
Woodbrook	Killian	234	17	177
Total		7,026	926	2,258

Source: Griffith's Valuation

* The remainder of these townlands were owned by other landlords.

The tenants' victory was only a temporary respite. On 25 November, the eviction party was back, this time composed of the sub-sheriff, bailiffs, 40 constables and 55 soldiers. This massive show of force was sufficient to ensure that the evictions were carried out and thus John Gerrard gained full possession of his newly purchased lands. The clearance at Kilcoosh is an interesting one for a number of reasons. By 1853, there was a formal mechanism in place for the reporting of evictions, resulting in more details and a clearer picture of their extent. Previously, the issuing of a notice to quit might have been the spur to encourage a recalcitrant tenant to do something about his arrears or on the other hand to meekly accept the notice and voluntarily vacate the premises. The evictions at Kilcoosh also indicate the depth of John Gerrard's commitment to grazing rather than tenancy. In 1853, he was 80 years of age, a time when most people are keenly aware of their own mortality. Nevertheless, his zeal for land clearance remained undiminished, adding some proof to a newspaper observation in the aftermath of the Ballinlass clearances: 'It is said that Mr or Mrs Gerrard (or both) have an uncontrollable fancy for converting tenanted lands into pasture.'[25] The Kilcoosh evictions are also significant in that for the first time on the Gerrard estate there was evidence of a formal organized resistance to an eviction. This perhaps was an early indication of some kind of a rural mobilization whose energy was later to be harnessed in the Land League.

The publication of Griffith's Valuation gave further insights into the extent of John Gerrard's clearances in his estate in the parishes of Ballynakill and Killian, both in the barony of Killian, County Galway. Table 3.1 shows the number of acres in each townland, the number of acres held by tenants, and the total valuation of each townland owned by John Gerrard in those parishes. The acreage has been rounded up or down, as appropriate, to the nearest acre. Similarly the valuation has been rounded up or down, as appropriate, to the nearest £.

Thus, by the mid-1850s, John Gerrard held 7,026 acres of which only 926 acres was leased to tenants. The remaining 6,100 acres were held 'in fee' by the landlord as grazing lands. This is a clear testament to the extent of his clearance policy. The existence on the same lands of 12 herds' houses, two stewards' houses and a woodsman's house offer further evidence of the extent of the depopulation of the lands. The average valuation over the whole estate was approximately 6s. 6d. per acre. The extent of demand for land in 1827 is clearly shown in that the Ballinlass tenants offered 30s. per acre, Irish measure, which would correspond to 18s. 6d. per statute acre, three times the valuation placed on it in the mid 1850s. This also offers a possible explanation for Mr Gerrard's tolerance towards the Ballinlass tenants until 1842. The lands were producing a regular and substantial return per acre and it was only when difficulties arose with the payment of rent that he took action. His own account of the years in question states that he 'remonstrated' with the tenants with regard to subletting – hardly a decisive course of action. The population returns for the three census years, 1841, 1851 and 1861 also offer an insight into Mr Gerrard's grazing policy. Table 3.2 shows the population of the Gerrard properties for the census years in question.

These returns indicate a dramatic drop of more than 50 per cent in the population of John and Marcella Gerrard's estate over a period of 20 years, brought about by a combination of aggressive land clearance and famine. From a perspective of more than 150 years later it is difficult to judge whether famine or land clearance had the greater impact. However a further analysis of the

Table 3.2. Population of Gerrard landholdings in Ballynakill and Killian
parishes, 1841–61

Townland	Parish	Population 1841	Population 1851	Population 1861
Ballinlass	Ballynakill	363	4	7
Carrownagappul	Ballynakill	90	24	21
Longford	Ballynakill	9	8	10
Ballynacorra	Killian	109	81	77
Ballynalaghy	Killian	0	5	14
Boherbannagh	Killian	72	53	29
Cloonavihony	Killian	271	150	120
Cloughbrack	Killian	94	55	67
Cloonkeen	Killian	2	3	6
Gunnode	Killian	301	92	70
Kilcoosh	Killian	270	202	7
Laghacrogher	Killian	116	5	0
Newbridge	Killian	56	25	7
Newgrove	Killian	7	7	20
Newvillage	Killian	6	8	0
Rushestown	Killian	330	344	367
Summerhill	Killian	0	0	0
Toghergar	Killian	6	7	4
Toomard	Killian	126	99	126
Tully	Killian	7	0	0
Windfield	Killian	18	19	13
Woodbrook	Killian	0	10	2
Total		2,253	1,201	967

Source: Census of Population 1861

population returns shows that by 1861, three townlands, Cloonavihony,
Rushestown and Toomard, contained a population of 613 persons,
approximately two-thirds of the entire estate, while the remaining 5,325 acres
of the estate had a population of 277 persons. This suggests that a policy of
land clearance was a major contributor to the depopulation of the estate.

An examination of the housing returns over the same 20-year period also
offers an insight into the situation. Table 3.3 shows the number of houses on
the estate in the period 1841–61.

Table 3.3. Number of houses on Gerrard landholdings in Ballynakill and Killian parishes, 1841–61

Townland	Parish	Houses 1841	Houses 1851	Houses 1861
Ballinlass	Ballynakill	66	1	1
Carrownagappul	Ballynakill	13	4	4
Longford	Ballynakill	1	1	1
Ballynacorra	Killian	20	15	14
Ballynalaghy	Killian	0	1	2
Boherbannagh	Killian	13	7	8
Cloonavihony	Killian	50	28	24
Cloughbrack	Killian	20	13	13
Cloonkeen	Killian	4	2	8
Gunnode	Killian	52	21	14
Kilcoosh	Killian	50	37	1
Laghacrogher	Killian	25	1	0
Newbridge	Killian	11	5	1
Newgrove	Killian	1	1	6
Newvillage	Killian	3	0	0
Rushestown	Killian	69	87	87
Summerhill	Killian	0	0	0
Toghergar	Killian	1	1	2
Toomard	Killian	20	24	30
Tully	Killian	1	0	0
Windfield	Killian	3	2	3
Woodbrook	Killian	1	2	1
Total		424	315	220

Source: Census of Population 1861

The population and housing returns tend to confirm the reports of evictions and demolition of houses at Ballinlass in 1846 and at Kilcoosh in 1853. The figures for the townland of Laghacrogher also suggest that it could have been the location of a clearance in 1848. The 1841 census shows a population of 116 residing in 25 houses, while the census of 1851 shows a population of five persons residing in one house. These statistics add some weight to the suggestion that it was the location of Connor/Corner village. This clearance is also reported in a report on the eviction of destitute persons in 1849.[26] The townland is named as 'Lacrogher' and a report of eight evictions was forwarded to the relieving officer at Ballinasloe workhouse, while a report of seven evictions was forwarded to the officer at Roscommon workhouse. In both cases the evictions were carried out on behalf of John N. Gerrard. No portion of this townland lay in the Roscommon union, so it is difficult to offer any explanation other than to minimize the extent of the clearance by dividing the report into two parts. In any event, the net result of John Gerrard's style of estate management was that, for the most part, his land was free of tenants so that he could pursue his 'uncontrollable fancy' for grazing land while restricting the majority of his tenantry to pockets of less valuable land.

The figures for the townland of Newbridge also appear to confirm the assertion of one of Redmond's interviewees that it had once been 'a rising village'.[27] The 1841 returns show a population of 56 persons resident in 11 houses. By 1851, this had fallen to a total of 25 persons residing in five houses and by 1861 this had dwindled to seven people resident in one house. At the same time, John and Marcella Gerrard had set about constructing a new village at the same location, though technically in the townland of Newgrove. This consisted of a market house, inn and a police barracks with accommodation for 12 constables. This new settlement was named Newtown Gerrard. It appears that the Gerrards also introduced a fair to the new village as national and provincial newspapers such as the *Freeman's Journal*, the *Tuam Herald* and the *Nenagh Guardian*, as well as *Thom's Directory* regularly advertised four fairs per year for Newtown Gerrard, Co. Galway. The earliest fair seems to have been held on 12 March 1841,[28] suggesting that the village of Newtown Gerrard had been constructed by then. This would also tally with the notice published in *The Nation* by Michael O'Connor stating that he had been a merchant of some standing at the Newbridge settlement at the same location. However, despite these efforts and considerable investment, the village of Newtown Gerrard was a commercial and social failure. The market house lay idle for many years; the barracks was never occupied by the constabulary, though the inn was for a time occupied by a Patrick Ginty, who also acted as a land steward for the Gerrards. Later developments were to invigorate the settlement, but by then the name of Newtown Gerrard had fallen into disuse and the older name of Newbridge had returned into usage.

In November 1858 the *Belfast News-Letter* reported the death on the 13th of that month, 'in the 86th year of his age, John Netterville Gerrard Esq, of Gibbstown, County Meath and Netterville, County Galway.'[29] The indications are that, with his death, there was an end to the aggressive clearance policy that he so devoutly espoused. Following his death, his widow Marcella appears to have continued the direct management of the estate. The following year, the society section of the *News-Letter* noted; 'Mrs Gerrard has returned to Gibbstown from Netterville.'[30] The notice contained no reference to the duration of her stay at Netterville Lodge. However, such an announcement in the society pages of a national newspaper would suggest a considerable absence from Gibbstown. Her death, intestate, on 18 November 1865, signaled the end of the Lecarrow/Longford branch of the Netterville family and opened a new chapter in the history of the estate.

John Gerrard's first encounter with his tenants at Ballinlass took place in 1827. By the time of his death, some 30 years later, he had converted some 6,000 acres of his wife's Galway estate to grazing pasture, while at the same time compressing his 800 tenants into less than 1,000 acres of mainly marginal land. One can only speculate why he did so. He and his wife had no heirs to succeed them. It appears that he was motivated solely by a desire to achieve maximum productivity from his land to the detriment of all other factors. He personified a clash of cultures between the 'village' or rundale system, where community welfare was paramount, and the view that 'private profit was a good and desirable thing in itself and not something which had to be subordinated to the good of the community as a whole.'[31] His commitment to the production of top quality livestock was evident from his many prize-winning exhibits at the Royal Dublin Society's spring show. His approach to the management of his estate was, perhaps, summed up by the *Daily News* with the observation:

> But Mr Gerrard is notoriously bent on bullock pastures, and has no taste at all for what the Yankees call 'humans' upon his estates; the humans bring neither high prices at Smithfield, nor prizes at cattle shows; bullocks are pasturing over half a dozen other villages de-populated – legally of course, by Mr Gerrard.[32]

It is likely that John Gerrard considered himself as an efficient, progressive farmer, and this progressive approach, as he saw it, overrode all humanitarian considerations and presumed on the landlords' right, in his view, to do with his lands as he saw fit.

4. The post-Famine years

The details of the 1851 census of population indicate that on his Galway estate, John Gerrard had, by then, all but achieved his goal of converting his land into a huge grazing farm. 6,000 acres had been de-tenanted and was populated mainly by the inhabitants of herds' houses, the herds being in his direct employment. Of the lands still occupied by tenants, three townlands, Cloonavihony, Rushestown and Toomard had a population of 593 persons, almost half the population of the entire estate.[1] The short-term capital requirements for the clearance and stocking of such a large land area were considerable. The legal costs involved in the eviction of tenants, as well as the employment of bailiffs, would also have been costly. In addition, the eviction of tenants almost invariably meant the foregoing of rent arrears which were due. An even greater capital cost was the purchase of stock to graze the thousands of acres in question. The raising of grazing stock was generally achieved in three phases. Calves or yearlings were purchased from dairy farms in Munster and grazed on land particularly in Galway and Roscommon until they were approximately two years old when they were transferred to the more fertile lands in Meath, Westmeath and Kildare for finishing. The fairs at Ballinasloe, particularly the great October fair, was of crucial importance in this chain of events, as was confirmed by Mr Gerrard of Gibbstown to Arthur Young in 1777.[2] However with the advent of steamships and later of railways, the transportation of live cattle became faster and less hazardous, and this led to a marked increase in the export of live cattle. In this regard, Seth Jones observes: 'However, an increasing proportion of store cattle in the latter half of the nineteenth century were never finished on the fattening pastures of Leinster, but were exported live, as forward stores or semi-fat cattle, to Scotland and the eastern counties of England'.[3]

It is most likely that John Gerrard availed of this growing market as his 1,000 acre demesne in Gibbstown would not have been able to sustain the number of store cattle raised on his Galway estate. While the capital cost was substantial, there were three factors which favoured his ability to meet these capital costs. First, the Irish economy recovered rapidly in the aftermath of the Famine and agricultural prices, especially those of livestock, rose substantially, as Moran observes: 'What was most unusual was that the post Famine period was one of high economic gains for farms with incomes greatly in excess of rents as a result of increased prices for agricultural produce.'[4] Gerrard's investment in livestock had the potential, therefore, to give a substantial return in a relatively short time. The agricultural recovery would have also benefited his remaining tenants, resulting in the prompt payment of rents. Given his previous history with tenants, it is highly unlikely that many of his remaining tenants would risk going into arrears even for a short time. Second, it can be assumed that the Gibbstown estate, shrewdly managed as it was for at least two generations of the Gerrard family, was a major provider of capital funds for the re-stocking of the Galway estate. His purchase of the townland of Kilcoosh for £2,700,[5] under the Encumbered Estates Act in 1852, indicated that his access to capital remained undiminished, despite the substantial costs of stocking his estate. It is unlikely that his wife was a significant contributor to any capital fund.

The terms of Edmond Netterville's codicil in 1776 had precluded Marcella from any inheritance other than 'a charge to the sum of three thousand pounds for such younger children of the said Frederick Netterville as shall be living at his death, and to be paid to them in equal shares at their respective ages of 21 years.'[6] In fact, all of Frederick's children achieved the age of 21 years so Marcella's share of the £3,000 would have been £500, a substantial sum in itself, but a paltry figure compared to the capital requirement for the re stocking of 6,000 acres. It is also unlikely that Marcella Netterville received a substantial marriage settlement. Her step-father, Elias Corbally, would have been expected to provide a substantial dowry on the occasion of the marriage of his daughter Louisa to James Plunkett, 7th Lord Killeen. It is unlikely that he felt obliged to show a similar generosity towards his step-daughter, the daughter of the irresponsible Frederick Netterville. Third, John Gerrard, unlike many graziers in his position, was in the fortunate position that he was the owner of the lands in question, and therefore not obliged to pay rent for his grazing land. His position was further strengthened by the fact that his home farm at Gibbstown was in an area far less affected by the Famine than the western counties.

John Gerrard's zeal for the clearance of land for grazing purposes did not extend to estate improvement *per se*. When giving evidence to the Devon Commission in 1844, his near neighbour Denis Kelly of Castle Kelly, Ballygar, five miles north-east of Netterville Lodge, deplored the practice of subletting, and the rundale system, noting 'where farms were held in rundale, we have got the greater part of them divided into separate holding, and have introduced green crops.'[7] However in response to a direct question regarding farms held in joint tenancy or in common, he admitted: 'but on properties around me there is a great deal, nearly all; for one that is not, there are ten that are.'[8] His neighbour, John Gerrard, was one of those landlords who still tolerated the rundale system. It was this system that he encountered at Ballinlass in 1828 and it was claimed by the tenants' attorney that he attempted to force them to deal with the existing tenants as best they could. By his own admission, his efforts to deal with multiple tenancies, was merely 'by remonstrances'.[9]

Even in the aftermath of his 1841–53 clearances, the practice of joint tenancies prevailed on the small portion of his estate which was actually tenanted. The townland of Rushestown is a case in point. The total area of the townland was just over 882 acres, of which 260 acres was bog. Within the townland were holdings referred to as 'villages', such as Ward's Village, Creaghan's Village, Dunn's Village and Doyle's Village. In the case of Ward's Village, there were 14 joint tenants holding a total of 102 acres. Of this, Bryan Ward held land to the value of £8 10s., the largest valuation of the group. He may have been the head tenant of the group, though his buildings valuation was a mere 10s. suggesting that his dwelling and out offices were of modest extent.

This pattern is also evident in the other 'villages' in the townland of Rushestown, suggesting that having cleared the lands that he wished to clear, John Gerrard prepared to tolerate the practice of joint tenancy, with its attendant patchwork of rundale plots, as long as the rent was paid. It is likely that the marginal quality of the land, so close to bog, was a contributory factor to such tolerance. This pattern of group leasing was not restricted to the Gerrard estate. Regarding the Bellew estate located at Mount Bellew, some three miles south-west of Netterville Lodge, Clarke notes; 'The majority of tenants belonged to groups leasing in partnership. No strict rules applied to the numbers involved, but usually a 'company' contained less than 10 individuals and the size of the holding was generally averaged between 10 and 20 acres per household.'[10] However, unlike the Gerrards, Mr Dillon Bellew was a resident landlord, and he ensured that such leases contained a clause which prevented subletting of any kind. John Gerrard's intolerance towards tenants was manifest in his newly purchased property at Kilcoosh in 1853, when along with the property he inherited a large number of tenants. His purchase of the 381 acres under the Encumbered Estates Act of 1849 gave him certain rights with regard to tenants, as Lane observes: 'The new owner inherited all the powers of the old owner subject to whatever tenant' rights were stated on the rental. He could evict tenants, distrain for arrears of rent and refuse to renew leases that ran out.'[11]

On a national level, by 1853 the flood of evictions which had begun before the Famine had greatly diminished. There were no official eviction figures before 1849 and the number of notices to quit that were issued are an unreliable guide, as the notice to quit was frequently a device employed by landlords to expedite the payment of rent. However official figures show that in 1850, 19,949 families were evicted of which 5,403 were readmitted as caretakers.[12] The large number of households not readmitted suggest that the purpose of most evictions was the clearance of the land for grazing as in the case of John Gerrard, or the 'striping' of land into larger holdings for re-letting to individual tenants. By 1853, the number of evictions had fallen to 4,833 households of which 1,213 were readmitted, suggesting that by then the post-Famine clearances were on the way to completion. The Kilcoosh eviction instigated by John Gerrard was a piece of unfinished business, made possible by the terms of the Encumbered Estates Act and was probably, from his perspective, too good an opportunity to miss.

The death of Marcella Netterville Gerrard in November 1865 raised questions regarding the inheritance of her substantial estate. By all accounts she died intestate, and as she and her late husband were childless, there was no obvious heir to their property. Neither did either of them have any surviving siblings, though Marcella did have two half siblings, Louisa and Matthew Corbally, the children of Marcella's mother, Mary Keogh and her second husband Elias Corbally. It appears that John Gerrard had made a will, leaving his Meath property to his nephew Thomas Gerrard, who promptly engaged the services of the well-known architect, William Henry Lynn, to construct a substantial mansion on the Gibbstown estate at a cost in excess of £70,000.[13] There was no record of a will by Marcella Gerrard and the fact that the residence on the Galway estate, Netterville Lodge, had rarely been occupied for many years, proved to be an irresistible temptation for a distant relative of hers. Geoffrey Davies was a landholder who held lands in the townland of Kentstown, adjacent to the Netterville estate. He had previously held lands in excess of 2,300 acres in a selection of townlands in the parish of Killian, adjacent to the Gerrard estate, but had been forced to offer them for sale in 1851 under the Encumbered Estates Act.[14] The sale of Davies' full estate did not succeed and part of it was later offered for sale a second time. John Gerrard purchased the townland of Kilcoosh in 1853, and promptly evicted the tenants. Davies was a distant relative of Marcella Gerrard. His great-grandfather was Nicholas Netterville of Longford, who had married twice. Marcella was a descendant of Nicholas by his first wife Mary Burke, while Davies was a descendant of Nicholas by his second wife, Mary Betagh. The relationship was distant to say the least; however Geoffrey Davies, obviously a supporter of the maxim that possession is nine points of the law, simply moved into Netterville Lodge and declared himself to be the rightful heir to Marcella Netterville Gerrard's property. To reinforce his newly acquired status he renamed himself as Netterville Davies. This action precipitated the emergence of a number of aspiring owners to the estate and of a dispute regarding ownership that was to be decided by the courts the following year. Most of the available information on this dispute comes from correspondence between another distant relative of Marcella Gerrard, Patrick Netterville, who resided in Ballygar, a town situated some six miles from Netterville Lodge, and Joshua McEvoy Netterville, son in law of James, 7th Viscount Netterville, another descendant of the Mary Betagh line of the family. The tone of the correspondence suggests that Patrick Netterville was in poor circumstances and hoped to benefit from Lady Netterville's accession to the property. The speed with which Davies acted is indicated by the contents of a letter that Patrick Netterville wrote to the viscountess on 28 November 1865, 10 days after the death of Marcella Gerrard and a mere six days after her death notice was published in a newspaper.[15] The extracts from Patrick Netterville's correspondence are presented in their original form without amendments to spelling, grammar or punctuation in order to preserve their authenticity. He wrote:

> My Lady,
>   I beg to State to you the transaction that has taken place here Since the death of Mrs Gerrard. Geffry Davis has taken forcible posession of her house, and is doing away with all her property, he auctioned off 25 head of cattle at yesterday of a place called Lowvill, My Brother and me went to the Lodge on yesterday and told Davis he acted illegal … if the chattle property is not looked after Davis will do away with them all, he has also broken open the cellar, and given drink to the whole country to keep up mob law, there is no time to be lost there should be instant steps taken to put down this usurper.[16]

The letter also referred to a visit to Netterville Lodge by Captain McEvoy who was the viscountess's son-in-law. This suggests that Joshua McEvoy and his wife Mary Netterville were already aware of Marcella's death, and the possibility of inheriting a substantial fortune. Patrick Netterville concluded his letter by offering his services to the viscountess 'and I shall feel pleasure in doing all that is best for the family.'[17] The evidence suggests that while Lady Netterville was aware that her late husband was related to Marcella Gerrard, she had no idea of the actual nature of the relationship. She delegated the investigation of the matter to her son-in-law Joshua McEvoy, who following his marriage to Lady Netterville's daughter Mary, had adopted the name Joshua McEvoy Netterville. One of Mr McEvoy Netterville's first courses of action was to consult Sir Bernard Burke of *Burke's peerage*, in order to establish the relationship. It was Sir Bernard who established that 'Marcella Gerrard and the seventh Viscount Netterville had shared a common ancestor in one Nicholas Netterville who had died in 1719 and whose father had been the third out of the seven sons of the first Viscount.'[18] This somewhat tenuous relationship was sufficient to occupy Mr McEvoy Netterville's energies for the next three months before he and his in-laws finally abandoned their quest for Netterville Lodge and the 7,000 acre estate on which it stood. However the correspondence generated by his quest casts a valuable light into the competition for the property. Given the childless marriage of John and Marcella Gerrard and also the lack of full siblings, it is likely that as they got older, there was much local speculation as to who would inherit the estate. Patrick Netterville's correspondence indicates that James, 7th Viscount Netterville, and his heirs were regarded as contenders. In a letter to Joshua McEvoy Netterville in December 1865, Patrick Netterville stated: 'the late Lord James told me he demanded the property of Mrs Gerrard, but that he would not disturb her during her life, and that nothing would keep it from him after her death'.[19] The same letter informed 'Mr Corbally took the Stock off the land on yesterday and brought them to the County Meath.'[20] It is presumed that the Mr Corbally referred to was Marcella Gerrard's half brother, Matthew Corbally. This indicates that he, and possibly his sister Louisa, the wife of Arthur James Plunkett, earl of Fingal, were also monitoring events in the aftermath of the death of their step-sister. The same letter also suggests that the youthful indiscretions of Marcella's father, Frederick Netterville, though committed in Dublin, were well known and had become part of local folklore. In a possible reference to the codicil which Edmond had added to his will, Patrick Netterville colourfully observed: 'the deed was passed to punish & disinherit his son Frederick in his anger, for marrying the actress Kitty Cutindash, he got himself divorced afterward from that marriage for which his father paid Kitty £5,000 he then got him married to a Miss Keogh.'[21] The same letter suggested that Frederick had also amassed debts of £3,574 17s. 10d. which had to be honoured by his exasperated father.

While Patrick Netterville proved to be a willing and prolific correspondent with Joshua McEvoy Netterville, there are some questions regarding his reliability. In a letter dated 27 January 1866, he acknowledged the receipt of half of a £10 note from Mr McEvoy, and three days later he acknowledged receipt of the second half of the note. It is entirely possible that Patrick was sending information that he thought McEvoy would wish to hear. Patrick himself also became involved in litigation with Geoffrey Davies, who, upon seizing Netterville Lodge, had styled himself as Netterville Davies. On 6 January 1866, Patrick reported to Joshua McEvoy Netterville that in mid-December 1865 he (Patrick) had received word that a consignment of goods had arrived at Roscommon railway station for 'Mr Netterville'. Patrick duly signed for the goods and took possession on the supposed assumption 'that you were the good donor who sent them to me as a Xmas present I then invited my friends and the principal tenants who were favourable to your cause on the Netterville property we regaled ourselves and consumed the goods as a God Send.'[22]

The fact that the goods had been consigned by Mssrs Gilby & Company gives an indication of their nature. The goods had been ordered by Geoffrey, now Netterville, Davies and he set about recovering their value. The ensuing case was subsequently reported in a local newspaper which noted that the 'goods' were indeed a consignment of whiskey and brandy ordered by a Ballygar shopkeeper, Mr Donovan, for 'Mr Geoffrey Davis, who since his accession to the Woodpark [sic] estates, has taken the name Netterville.'[23] The paper noted that the case stood over for trial at petty session and 'the prisoner, being admitted to bail, offered to make good the loss by every means in his power.'[24] In mid-January of 1866, Patrick Netterville mournfully appraised Joshua McEvoy of the outcome of the trial, observing 'there was never such a bench of magistrates in Roscommon as collected on that occasion for my conviction, nine in number with Lord Crofton as their chairman.'[25] He reported that he was charged with larceny and offered to 'compromise with the Station Master for £33 giving him approved bills for that amount payable in 6 months and 9 months, that ends this great trial, memorable as it will be in Roscommon for years to come.'[26] If things looked bad for Patrick Netterville on that day, they were about to get worse, as the following month he received correspondence from Joshua McEvoy that he and his in-laws had given up their pursuit of Marcella Gerrard's estate. Patrick's response gives an indication of his dismay as he observed regarding receipt of the letter, 'it has nearly parilize my energy for since my boyhood, I believed that Lord James and his successors would possess the property after the death of Mrs Gerrard'.[27] He concluded the letter by begging Mr McEvoy not to give up the struggle.

The withdrawal of Lady Netterville and her daughters left three other parties, including Geoffrey Davies, in contention for the estate. Surprisingly, the contenders did not include either of Marcella Gerrard's half siblings, Matthew or Louisa Corbally. This may suggest that they were aware of the codicil attached to Edmond Netterville's will in 1776 disinheriting Frederick Netterville and his successors. The terms of the will also question Marcella Netterville's right to the estate in the first place. Had she not married the formidable John Gerrard, it is possible that her right to the estate would have been questioned long before 1865. The two parties who instituted a legal challenge to Geoffrey Davies' acquisition of the estate were Arthur James Netterville, of Cruicerath, Co. Meath, and John Fallon of Runnymeade, Co. Roscommon. John Fallon was a descendant of Margaret, sister of Edmond Netterville of Longford (Co. Galway) and Glasnevin, Marcella Netterville Gerrard's grandfather. Arthur James Netterville was a descendant of Cecilia, also a sister of Edmond Netterville. Arthur James was, in 1867, to successfully claim the title of 8th Viscount Netterville in a house of lords enquiry. The case taken by the plaintiffs was heard at Galway assizes in March 1866, and judging by newspaper reports, attracted considerable attention. The *Galway Vindicator* noted: 'The case attracted great attention from the magnitude of the interests involved. The grand jury box was occupied by ladies, and the court was thronged with anxious listeners.'[28] The article went on to describe the extent of the late Marcella Netterville Gerrard's estates in Meath and Galway, suggesting that she had 'left personalty to the amount, it is stated, of £300,000, which goes between her next of kin, the Countess of Fingal and Mr Corbally of Corbalton Hall in the county of Meath'.[29] This suggests that Mrs Gerrard's financial legacy went to her half siblings and begs the question as to why her landed estate did not follow in a similar direction. It seems reasonable to conclude that she had knowledge of her grandfather's codicil, and was aware that for some 60 years she had little more than caretaker status on the Netterville estate. Matthew Corbally MP, Marcella's half brother, also gave evidence at the hearing. He confirmed 'my mother's name was Mary Keogh, the widow of Frederick Netterville of Longford: they had a residence called Woodbrook. I know all the children of the first marriage … the three sisters lived at my father's house.'[30] He confirmed the death of Marcella's sister Maria in 1823 and that of her sister Cressey in 1824. The presence of Mr Corbally at the hearing as a witness, further suggests that Mrs Gerrard's half siblings were not themselves claimants for the property in question. The legal team representing the plaintiffs 'produced the will of Mr Netterville and other documents from the House of Lords'.[31]

It was fortunate for the plaintiffs, that, for an entirely different reason, the will of Edmond Netterville of Longford was read, in its entirety, into the record of a house of lords enquiry in July 1830.[32] The enquiry was set up to investigate the claims of James Netterville of Frahane, Co. Mayo, to the honour and title of 7th Viscount Netterville, which had become vacant due to the death, without issue, of John, the 6th viscount in 1826. James Netterville and Marcella Gerrard shared a common ancestor in Nicholas Netterville of Lecarrow, Co. Galway, grandson of Nicholas Netterville of Dowth, the 1st Viscount Netterville. Marcella was a descendant of Nicholas Netterville and his first wife Mary Burke, while James was descended from Nicholas and his second wife Mary Betagh. It seems that in his claim for the title, it was incumbent on James to show that the lineage from Nicholas and Mary Burke had no remaining claim to the title. The enquiry heard witnesses who testified to the death of the various male Netterville aspirants to the title of viscount. The thrust of the enquiry suggests that had he survived, Edmond Netterville of Longford and his male descendants would have succeeded to the title. However, the death of Edmond Netterville in 1777 and that of his only son Frederick in 1785, followed by the deaths of all three of Frederick's sons in the early years of the 19th century ended the title claims of that branch of the family. Had Frederick or any of his three sons survived the 6th viscount, it would have been an interesting question regarding the claim of a disinherited son or grandson on the title of Viscount Netterville. In any event, the enquiry confirmed the deaths of Marcella Netterville Gerrard's three brothers and also revealed the contents of Edmond Netterville's will of 1765 and the amending codicil of 1776. The original will, though lengthy, was straightforward. The property was bequeathed to 'the use of my first and every other son & heirs male of the body & bodies of such son & sons, according to the priority of birth, the elder of such son and sons, and the heirs male of his body, always to be preferred to the younger'.[33] The will went on to specify who should 'in default of such issue' inherit the estate. The exhaustive list began with Edmond's grandson, Peter Lawerence, son of Margery, sister of Edmond Netterville. It appears that neither fertility nor longevity were traits of the male Netterville line, with the result that most of the proposed beneficiaries of Edmond's will had no male heirs by 1865. Thus when Marcella Netterville Gerrard died, she had no close relatives other than her half-siblings Matthew Corbally and Louisa Lady Killeen.

The production of Edmond Netterville's will at the Galway assizes on 24 March 1866 appears to have satisfied the jury regarding the outcome of the case made by the plaintiffs. When the court resumed on Monday, 26 March, Mr Isaac Butt QC 'concluded his address for the defendant and produced the will by which the defendant got possession.'[34] There is no indication as to what kind of will Mr Butt produced on behalf of his client Geoffrey Davies, but it cut little ice with the jurors who 'after a quarter of an hour's deliberation found a verdict for the plaintiffs.'[35] Geoffrey Davies' bold attempt to acquire the estate ended in failure, resulting in his removal from Netterville Lodge and the division of the estate into three parts. A contemporary publication showed that Arthur James, 8th Viscount Netterville held 1,713 statute acres; John Fallon held 2,594 acres while Sir John Bradstreet held 2,496 acres.[36] Sir John Bradstreet was not listed as a plaintiff in the case. However he was a descendant of Bridget, a third sister of Edmond Netterville of Longford and Glasnevin and, as such, was judged to be entitled to one-third of the estate.

Of the three beneficiaries, only John Fallon became a resident landlord. He took up residence in Netterville Lodge and by all accounts established a reputation as a fairer landlord than his predecessor. By 1870 he had donated a parcel of land for the construction of a Catholic chapel at Newtown Gerrard. In fact the chapel incorporated the disused market house that had been constructed by John Gerrard in or about 1840. The construction of the church began the revival of Newtown Gerrard as a population settlement. By then it had almost certainly reverted to its former name, Newbridge, as the name imposed on it by the landlord was never fully embraced by the local people. However the list of fairs and markets continued to advertise five fairs per year in Newtown Gerrard until 1884. Significantly the directory also indicated three fairs for Newbridge in 1883 and 1884. After 1884 there were no further entries for fairs at Newtown Gerrard and it can be assumed that by then the name of the settlement was universally accepted as Newbridge.

The fate of the victims of John Gerrard's clearance policy is unclear. The poor and dispossessed leave little trace in the surviving evidence, other than

4 Netterville Lodge.

in statistical reports and returns. One can only speculate as to how they and their hundreds of thousands of counterparts survived. The options were limited and stark. Those who were ready and willing to pay their rent had the option of seeking to start again by renting land from a more accommodating landlord. This was a possibility in the post-Famine years when the population had diminished and land was available at more modest rents. However, the parcels of land on offer would have been bigger as landlords were unlikely to become involved in the letting of tiny patches of land as had previously been the case. In addition, the post-Famine period saw the rundale, or 'village' system, grow further into disrepute, so the prospective tenant was faced with working and living on his own holding of land.

There was no suggestion of any landlord-assisted emigration scheme on the estate, despite the fact that it had been availed of by tenants of Sir Robert Gore Booth's Sligo estate as early as 1839, when; 'Forty-two families, comprising 207 individuals, accepted Sir Robert's offer of assisted passage in 1839 and 1841 and received potatoes and other provisions for the sea journey.'[37] Indeed it was said that John Gerrard, when advised to consider this by his landlord neighbours, dismissed the suggestion out of hand. Thus if his former tenants did emigrate they did so at their own expense, limiting this option to those who could afford it. The workhouse in Ballinasloe was another option available to the Gerrard tenantry and it is likely that some reluctantly availed of its provisions. The fact that workhouses were constructed at Mount Bellew and Glenaddy in a second phase of workhouse provision suggests that the local demand for workhouse accommodation in the area was considerable. The Mount Bellew poor law union participated in at least one assisted emigration venture when it contributed £1 each towards the emigration of thirty females to Tasmania. The minutes noted that the emigration agent representing the Colonial Land and Emigration Commissioners 'has selected 30 of the female inmates for passage to Van Diemen's Land by the ship "*Travencore*" which will sail from Plymouth on 23 inst.'[38] Contemporary reports of the Ballinlass clearance suggested that the evictees were walking the roads, living in ditches and begging for food. Newspapers reported the deaths of two of the evictees, Lacky Rock and Pat Gibbons, in Mount Bellew in 1846 and 1847 respectively.

A survivor of the Ballinlass evictions wrote to her niece in the United States in 1908. Bridget Mitchell was the daughter of Thady Gilmartin, whose household of eight people was evicted. Census returns indicate that she lived in the townland of Tonnacorra in the parish of Killian in 1901 and 1911 and would have been 12 years of age at the time of the evictions.[39] It is evident from her letter that the folk memory of the evictions was deeply ingrained into her consciousness. She referred to the death of the 'landlord who owned (Ballinlass) our old home' and continued:

> the members of Parliament who is fighting for Ireland's rights is getting the government of England to divide those lands from which the people were evicted and make them into holdings of 25 acres of land and every tenant who still lives will get the very land from which they were evicted and when that soon comes to pass I expect to have our home in the very spot where your mother aunt Maggie and myself were born.[40]

It is debatable if those were realistic expectations, yet they may have been shared by others in the same situation, indicating that more than 60 years later, the sense of injustice in the locality remained strong.

For the remaining tenants on the estate, life under new landlords continued as before. The clearances had largely been completed and the new owners did not appear to have any great appetite to extend the grazing farms. However, landlord-tenant relations were not universally cordial. John Fallon was involved in litigation with tenants of Lord Netterville who were cutting turf on his (Fallon's) lands at Kilcoosh in 1874.[41] Lord Netterville himself brought an ejectment decree for overholding against a group of his tenants at Ardeevan, in 1870.[42] These incidents suggest that while in general an uneasy peace had settled on the former Gerrard estate there were occasional outbreaks of hostility. The year 1870 also saw the introduction of Gladstone's Land Act. While its provisions fell short of Irish tenant expectations, it did begin the granting of some tenant rights, a process that was to be incrementally more favourable to those who worked the land than those who owned it.

Conclusion

The clearances effected by John Gerrard on his Galway estate between 1822 and 1858 were substantial and far reaching. His marriage to Marcella Netterville in 1822 sparked a chain of events which were to transform the structure of her substantial landholding in east Galway. It would appear that whereas her grandfather, Edmond Netterville, had been actively involved in the management of his estates, this active management did not continue following his death. The administrators of the estate seem to have had a *laissez faire* approach, which permitted subletting and sub-division as long as the rent was paid. The rapid rise in population and the consequent demand for land exacerbated an already difficult situation and it was in these circumstances that John Gerrard became beneficial owner of the lands in question. His acceptance of a proposal from the Ballinlass tenants in 1828 suggests that at that stage he too was prepared to tolerate subletting as long as the rent was paid. However, it appears that his resolve to convert his wife's land into a grazing farm similar to his own farm at Gibbstown, Co. Meath, grew strongly through the 1830s and 1840s. His adoption of a grazing policy resulted in the removal of hundreds of families from their meagre holdings without any attempt at relocation. His eviction of at least 69 families, comprising 270 persons, and the demolition of their houses at Ballinlass on 13 March 1846, was one of the largest clearances of the Famine era. By the time of his death in 1858, some 6,000 acres were left free of tenants and available for the grazing of his livestock. It is clear that these actions had a profound and varying impact on the structure of the estate. While many townlands were stripped free of tenants, there was a sizeable increase in the population of those townlands he chose to leave undisturbed. The population of the townlands of Rushestown and Toomard actually increased between 1851 and 1861. On the other hand townlands such as Ballinlass, Kilcoosh, Lahacrogher and Newbridge were all but depopulated.

This depopulation caused social and cultural upheaval, interfering with the social fabric of the community where kinship and neighbourly support were part of the way of life. It is likely that this upheaval also hastened the decline of the Irish language in the area, as emigration would have been forced on at least some of the evictees, making the learning of English all but essential for life in Britain, the United States or Canada. Many questions remain unanswered regarding the fate of those who were evicted and had their dwellings destroyed. It seems reasonable to assume that some of those who were ready and willing to pay their rent were accommodated as tenants on other landed estates, while those who could not afford to do so had few options other than the workhouse. Emigration required capital, particularly in the absence of a sponsored emigration scheme. Nevertheless, correspondence from one of the Ballinlass evictees to her niece in the United States confirms that the emigrant ship was availed of by at least one of the evictees and it seems reasonable to speculate that more than one person availed of this. Similarly the deaths of Lacky Rock and Pat Gibbons, coupled with the Famine reports of the Ballynakill curate, Fr Mcloughlin, confirm that some of the victims of John Gerrard's clearances did not survive his heartless actions. The creation of a new poor law union in Mount Bellew and the provision of a workhouse there in 1848 further suggest a large increase in the demand for indoor relief in the years 1846–53. The Famine was undoubtedly a major cause of this demand; however, it is likely that the Gerrard clearances were also a significant contributory factor. That the poor law union sponsored emigration of 50 girls from Mount Bellew workhouse, aged between 15 and 30 years, in 1853 also suggests the possibility that some of the Gerrard tenants were included.

While John Gerrard was somewhat ahead of his landlord peers in his view that tenants were a barrier to agricultural improvement, his clearances must be also viewed in a national context of widespread clearances in the years 1845–53. Absence of constabulary eviction returns in the years up to 1849 precludes any definitive figure, and there is much debate among historians regarding the actual number of evictions in the period. Mary Daly suggests that 3,500–3,600 families were evicted in 1846, while W.E. Vaughan estimates a figure of 24,092 in the years 1846–8. The first official figures were in 1849 when 16,686 evictions were recorded. The Gerrard clearances were an early example of a nationwide phenomenon in the years 1840–53. There were widespread clearances in Clare and Mayo during the period in question. In the parish of Ballinrobe, Lord Lucan, who had said that he would not breed paupers to pay priests, evicted some 2,000 people between 1846 and 1849. Donnelly's observation in this regard offers a chilling echo of the actions of John Gerrard: 'The depopulated holdings, after being consolidated, were sometimes retained and stocked by Lord Lucan himself as grazing farms and in other cases were leased as ranches to wealthy graziers.'[1] What is clear is that the eviction of tenants was widely used as an instrument of land clearance, and landowners such as John Gerrard were in the vanguard of such clearances.

The death of John Gerrard in 1858 brought an end to the aggressive policy of clearance for grazing that he had so actively promoted. The meagre sources available offer little insight into his widow's approach or involvement in the estate in her declining years other than the fact that she was at least an occasional visitor to Netterville Lodge. The break-up of the estate after her death meant that there were three new landlords, John Fallon, Sir John Valentine Bradstreet, and Arthur James, 8th Viscount Netterville. Of these only

John Fallon became a resident landlord. A Catholic, he facilitated the provision of a Catholic church in Newbridge. This church, which still serves the Newbridge community, incorporates the market house which was built by John Gerrard in his attempt to create the village of Newtown Gerrard.

The arrival of three new landlords did not necessarily result in an immediate and lasting improvement in landlord-tenant relations. Viscount Netterville issued an ejectment decree for overholding on a group of tenants in Ardeevan in 1870.[2] John Fallon was also involved in a dispute with a group of Viscount Netterville's tenants. He, accompanied by his herd, accosted the group cutting turf on his lands at Kilcoosh in June 1874. They indicated that they had always cut their turf there in Mrs Gerrard's time and forcefully voiced their intentions of continuing the practice.[3] A shooting incident at Woodbrook in 1879, involving Peter Bartleman, a grazier tenant of Viscount Netterville, adds further evidence that the resentment towards grazing and graziers continued well beyond the time of the Gerrard ownership and provided fertile ground for cultivation of the aspirations of the Land League.[4]

Gladstone's land act of 1870 fell far short of tenant expectations; nevertheless it was the beginning of a process leading towards the redistribution of the land of Ireland on a more equitable basis. Thus it can be argued that it presaged the end of a landlord-tenant relationship in which the landlord was the dominant partner. The decades in which John Gerrard held a beneficial interest in the Netterville estate were a period of profound change, during which global economic trends impacted at local level and transformed agricultural practices and local economies. His response to those economic trends coupled with the devastation of the Famine years left a long lasting imprint on the parishes of Ballynakill and Killian.

Appendix 1. Families evicted at Ballinlass, 13 March 1846

Name	No. in household	Name	No. in household
Bryan, Matthew	6	Gavin, Widow	5
Callaghan, John	2	Geoghagan, Billy	2
Cheevers, Michael	7	Gibbons, Pat	1
Clarke, Michael	5	Gilmartin, Thady	8
Conlan, John	6	Hegan, James	2
Conlan, Thady	7	Higgins, Pat	6
Conner, Bryan	6	Kelly, Thomas	3
Conroy, Pat	5	Kenny, Widow	4
Crehan, Larry	6	Kenny, Widow	3
Croghan, Widow	3	Kilmartin, Laurence	7
Daly, Widow	3	Loftus, Mark	3
Dillon, John	6	Manahan, John	8
Discon, Billy	4	Mantron, Patrick	5
Discon, Widow	5	Monaghan,	4
Driscol, Patrick	6	Morris	5
Egan, James	5	Morrissey, Pat	4
Finnerty, Andy	3	Mulrey, Michael	4
Flaherty, John	4	Murray, ——	4
Flymings, Pat	3	Murray, Widow	4
Forcy, Roger	5	Neill, Pat	9
Gavin, James	6	Norton, John	1
Gavin, John	3	Norton, Thomas	1
Gavin, Luke	8	O'Hara, Widow	4
Gavin, Mark	3	Rock, Laurence	5
Gavin, Michael	3	Rock, Michael	5
Gavin, Pat	3	Rock, Thady	4
Gavin, Pat	2	Rogerson, Pat	6
Gavin, Thomas	8	Smyth, Ned	5
Gavin, Thomas	7	Tansey, Thomas	4
Gavin, Tadhg	1	Walsh, John	2
Gavin, Tom	4		

Total families: 61   **Total persons: 270**

Source: Freeman's Journal, 27 Mar. 1846

Appendix 2. Families evicted at Connor/ Corner village, November 1848

Name	No. in household
Boyle, Thomas	1
Brehany, Patt	5
Connor, John	5
Connolly, Owen	4
Craghan, Owen	1
Crehan, Matthias	4
Crehan, Matty	8
Crehan, Owen	6
Haverty, Thomas	8
Mannion, Widow	3
Mee, Widow	6
Quinn, Martin	4
Quinn, William	1
Smith, Pat	5
Tarl, William	6

Total families: 15   **Total persons: 67**

Source: Freeman's Journal, 9 Nov. 1848

Notes

ABBREVIATIONS

CSORP   Chief Secretary's office, registered papers
Devon Commission   *Evidence taken before her majesty's commission of enquiry into the*
                         state of the law and practice in respect to the occupation of land in
                         Ireland, HC 1845 (605), XIX
Griffith's Valuation   *General valuation of rateable property in Ireland*
HC   House of Commons
HL   House of Lords
NAI   National Archives of Ireland
NLI   National Library of Ireland
RD   Registry of Deeds

INTRODUCTION

1 David Seth Jones, *Graziers, land reform,*
   and political conflict in Ireland
   (Washington, 1995).
2 W.E. Vaughan, *Landlords and tenants in*
   mid-Victorian Ireland (Oxford, 1994).
3 Timothy P. O'Neill, 'Famine evictions'
   in Carla King (ed.), *Famine, land and*
   culture in Ireland (Dublin, 2000), p. 48.
4 James S. Donnelly, 'Landlords and
   tenants,' in W.E. Vaughan (ed.), *A new*
   history of Ireland, v: Ireland under the
   Union (Oxford, 1989), p. 343.
5 Gerard P. Moran, *Sending out Ireland's*
   poor: assisted emigration to North America
   in the nineteenth century (Dublin, 2004),
   p. 23.
6 Gerard P. Moran, *Sir Robert Gore Booth*
   and his landed estate in County Sligo,
   1814–76: land, famine, emigration and
   politics (Dublin, 2006).
7 Liam Dolan, *Land war and eviction in*
   Derryveagh, 1840–65 (Dundalk, 1980).
8 Gerard P. Moran, *The Mayo evictions of*
   1860: Patrick Lavelle and the 'War' in
   Partry (Mayo, 1986).
9 Karen Jeanne Harvey, *The Bellews of*
   Mount Bellew: a Catholic gentry family in
   eighteenth century Ireland (Dublin, 1998).
10 Joe Clarke, *Christopher Dillon Bellew and*
   his Galway estates, 1763–1826 (Dublin,
   2003).

11 Anne Coleman, *Riotous Roscommon:*
   social unrest in the 1840s (Dublin, 1999),
   p. 17
12 Arthur Young, *A tour in Ireland with*
   general observations on the present state of
   that kingdom, made in the years 1776, 1777
   and 1778, 2 vols (London, 1792).
13 Samuel Lewis, *A topographical dictionary*
   of Ireland, 3 vols (London, 1837).
14 S. Redmond, *Landlordism in Ireland:*
   letters on the eviction of the Gerrard
   tenantry, a portion of which appeared
   originally in the Freeman's Journal
   (Dublin, 1846).

1. A GATHERING STORM

1 John Gough Nichols (ed.), *The herald*
   and genealogist (London, 1867), p. 545.
2 Robert C. Simington (ed.), *The*
   transplantation to Connacht, 1654–58
   (Shannon, 1970).
3 Will of Edmond Netterville, 15
   November 1765, and codicil attached,
   11 Apr. 1776 (NAI, 999/658/1).
4 Will and codicil of Edmond Netterville
   (NAI, 999/658/1).
5 David Synnott, 'Marcella Gerard's
   estate', *Journal of the Galway*
   Archaeological and Historical Society, 57
   (2005), 44.
6 Will and codicil of Edmond Netterville
   (NAI, 999/658/1).

7　Will and codicil of Edmond Netterville (NAI, 999/658/1).

8　http//churchrecords.irishgenealogy.ie/churchrecords/details/c7232270358043, accessed 14 Apr. 2011.

9　Gearóid Ó Tuathaigh, *Ireland before the Famine, 1798–1848* (Dublin, 1971), p. 34.

10　Oliver McDonagh, 'Ireland under the Union' in W.E.Vaughan (ed.), *A new history of Ireland* v (Oxford, 1989), introduction, p. xxix.

11　S.J. Connolly, 'Aftermath and adjustment' in *A new history of Ireland*, v, p. 170.

12　Anne Coleman, *Riotous Roscommon: social unrest in the 1840s* (Dublin, 1999), p. 16.

13　S.J. Connolly, 'The Catholic question' in *A new history of Ireland*, v, p. 26.

14　Ó Tuathaigh, *Ireland before the Famine*, p. 128.

15　Cormac Ó Gráda, 'Poverty, population and agriculture 1802–45' in *A new history of Ireland*, v, p. 118.

16　C. Woodham-Smith, *The great hunger: Ireland 1845–1849* (London, 1962), p. 20.

17　Ó Tuathaigh, *Ireland before the Famine*, p. 149.

18　Oliver McDonagh, 'Irish emigration to the United States of America and the British colonies during the Famine' in R. Dudley Edwards & T. Desmond Williams (eds), *The Great Famine* (Dublin 1997), p. 332.

19　*Nenagh Guardian*, 8 Aug. 1846.

20　*Kilkenny Journal*, 30 Sept. 1846.

21　Gerard Moran, *Sir Robert Gore Booth and his landed estates in County Sligo, 1814–1876* (Dublin, 2006), p. 37.

22　Patrick K. Egan, *The parish of Ballinasloe: its history from the earliest times to the present day* (Dublin, 1960), p. 240

23　Mary E. Daly, *The famine in Ireland* (Dundalk, 1986), p. 47.

24　Ó Gráda, 'Poverty population and agriculture', p. 123.

25　Ó Gráda, 'Poverty, population and agriculture', p. 126.

26　Henry Coulter, *The west of Ireland* (London, 1862), p. 9.

27　Ó Gráda, 'Poverty, population and agriculture', p. 133.

28　*Evidence taken before her majesty's commission of enquiry into the state of law and practice in respect to the occupation of land in Ireland*, HC 1845 (605), xix

(hereinafter referred to as the *Devon commission*), pt ii, p. 515, q. 6.

29　*Devon commission*, pt ii, p.529, q. 38.

30　*Devon Commission*, pt ii, pp 339–45, qs 4–74.

31　*Devon commission*, pt ii, pp339–45, qs 4–74.

32　*Devon commission*, pt ii, pps 36–7, q. 8.

33　Richard Griffith, *General valuation of rateable property in Ireland* (Dublin: Irish Microfilms, 1978).

34　Arthur Young, *A tour in Ireland with general observations on the present state of that kingdom, made in the years 1776, 1777 and 1778*, 2 vols (London 1892), i, p. 49.

35　Young, *A tour in Ireland*, i, p. 50.

36　Ibid.

37　Jim Gilligan, *Graziers and grasslands: portrait of a rural Meath community, 1854–1914* (Dublin, 2003), p. 29.

2. 'AWFUL EXTERMINATION OF TENANTRY'

1　T.W. Freeman, *Pre-Famine Ireland; a study in historical geography* (Manchester, 1957), p. 73.

2　Freeman, *Pre-Famine Ireland*, p. 243.

3　Figures extracted from census 1841.

4　Marriage settlement, John Gerrard & Marcella Netterville, 28 November 1822, RD 777/164/526299.

5　*Saunder's Newsletter*, 1 Apr. 1846.

6　*Roscommon Journal*, 4 Apr. 1846.

7　NAI, CSORP, Galway 184611/10561–11/19799.

8　*Saunders' Newsletter*, 1 Apr. 1846.

9　*Roscommon Journal*, 4 Apr. 1846.

10　*Saunder's Newsletter*, 1 Apr. 1846.

11　*The Nation*, 31 Jan. 1843.

12　*Freeman's Journal*, 27 Mar. 1846.

13　*Saunder's Newsletter*, 1 Apr. 1846.

14　S. Redmond, *Landlordism in Ireland, letters on the eviction of the Gerrard tenantry, a portion of which appeared originally in the Freeman's Journal* (Dublin, 1846), p. 2.

15　Redmond, *Landlordism in Ireland*, p. 2.

16　*Roscommon Journal*, 14 Mar. 1846.

17　*Galway Vindicator*, 28 Mar. 1846.

18　Ibid.

19　Redmond, *Landlordism in Ireland*, p. 4.

20　Ibid., p. 6.

21　Thomas Bermingham, 'The labourer makes the value of the land' in *Facts and illustrations for the labourer's friend society* (London, 1835).

22 Constabulary report on the Ballinlass evictions (NAI, CSORP, Galway 1846, 11/10561–11/19799).
23 Ibid.
24 Redmond, *Landlordism in Ireland*, p. 8.
25 Ibid.
26 *Freeman's Journal*, 2 Apr. 1846.
27 Redmond, *Landlordism in Ireland*, p. 29.
28 Ibid., p. 40.
29 *Roscommon Journal*, 4 Apr. 1846.
30 Redmond, *Landlordism in Ireland*, p. 38.
31 Ibid., p. 39.
32 Ibid., p. 47.
33 Ibid., p. 49.
34 *Saunder's Newsletter*, 1 Apr. 1846.
35 *Roscommon Journal*, 4 Apr. 1846.
36 *Saunder's Newsletter*, 4 Apr. 1846.
37 L. Perry Curtis Jr, *The depiction of eviction in Ireland, 1845–1910* (Dublin, 2011), p. 320.
38 *Roscommon Journal*, 4 Apr. 1846.
39 *Saunders' News-Letter*, 1 Apr. 1846.
40 Redmond, *Landlordism in Ireland*, p. 6.

3. AN UNCONTROLLABLE FANCY FOR PASTURE

1 *Freeman's Journal*, 2 Apr. 1846.
2 *Belfast News-Letter*, 7 Apr. 1846.
3 *Belfast News-Letter*, 7 Apr. 1846.
4 *The Times*, 6 Apr. 1846.
5 *The Times*, 9 Apr. 1846.
6 *The Times*, 9 Apr. 1846.
7 Mc Gregor, 26 March 1846 (NAI, CSORP, Galway, 1846, 11/10199).
8 *Freeman's Journal*, 13 May 1846.
9 *Hansard 3*, Ejectment of tenantry, Ireland, HC debate, 2 April 1846, vol. 85, cc 485–489.
10 Hansard 3, *Ejectment of tenantry, Ireland*, HC debate, 2 April 1846, vol. 85, cc 490.
11 Hansard, HL debate, 30 Mar. 1846, vol. 85, cc 273–8.
12 Hansard, HL debate, 3 Apr. 1846, vol. 85, cc 491–2.
13 *Nenagh Guardian*, 23 May 1846.
14 *Freeman's Journal*, 22 May 1846.
15 *The Times*, 6 May 1847.
16 *The Nation*, 24 Apr. 1847.
17 *Freeman's Journal*, 5 May 1847.
18 Ibid.
19 *Tuam Herald*, 11 Nov. 1848.
20 Interview with John Joe Crehan, Cloonavihony, Newbridge, Co. Galway, 24 Aug. 2011.
21 *Census of Ireland 1861: part 1. Area, population and number of houses, by townlands and electoral divisions provinces of Ulster and Connaught*, HC, 1863 [3204], lv, 391.
22 *Sale of rental of the lands of Ballinacor, Bugganes, Kilclough, Creveroe and Kilcoosh* (NAI, Landed estate court rentals (O'Brien), microfilm 391/3).
23 Constabulary report on Kilcoosh evictions, 11 Nov. 1853 (NAI, CSORP, Galway 1853, 10334/409).
24 Constabulary report on Kilcoosh evictions, 11 Nov. 1853 (NAI, CSORP, Galway, 1853, 10334/479).
25 *The Examiner* (London) 28 Mar. 1846.
26 *Evicted Destitute Poor(Ireland) Act. Abstract return of all notices served upon relieving officers of poor law districts in Ireland, by landowners and others, under the act 11 & 12 Vict. C. 47, intituled, an act for the protection and relief of the destitute poor evicted from their dwelling*, 4, [1089], HC, 1849, xlix, 282.
27 Redmond, *Landlordism in Ireland*, p. 49.
28 *Freeman's Journal*, 6 Mar. 1841.
29 *Belfast News-Letter*, 24 Nov. 1858.
30 *Belfast News-Letter*, 15 July 1859.
31 Raymond D. Crotty, *Irish agricultural production; its volume and structure* (Cork, 1966), p. 33.
32 *Daily News* (London), 8 Apr. 1846.

4. THE POST-FAMINE YEARS

1 *Census of Ireland 1851: part 1, Area, population and number of houses, by townlands and electoral divisions, county of Galway*, [1557], HC, 1852–3, xcii, 382–3.
2 Arthur Young, *A tour in Ireland with general observations on the present state of that kingdom, made in the years 1777, 1778 and 1779* (2 vols, London 1892), i, p. 39.
3 David Seth Jones, *Graziers, land reform and political conflict in Ireland* (Washington, 1995), pp 5–6.
4 Gerard P. Moran, *A radical priest in Mayo: Fr Patrick Lavelle: the rise and fall of an Irish nationalist, 1825–86* (Dublin, 1994), p. 128.
5 Padraig G. Lane, 'The encumbered estates court and Galway land ownership' in Gerard Moran (ed.), *Galway history and society* (Dublin, 1996), p. 403.
6 Manuscript copy, will of Edmond Netterville, 15 November 1765, and

codicil attached, 11 Apr., 1776 (NAI, 99/658/1).

7 *Devon commission*, ii, p. 339 [616] HC, 1845, q. 7.

8 *Devon commission* ii, p.340 [616], HC, 1845, q. 21.

9 *Saunder's News-Letter*, 1 Apr. 1846.

10 Joe Clarke, *Christopher Dillon Bellew and his Galway estates, 1763–1826* (Dublin, 2003), p. 22.

11 Padraig G. Lane, 'The general impact of the encumbered estates act of 1849 on counties Galway and Mayo', *Journal of the Galway Archaeological and Historical Society*, 33 (1972–3), 46.

12 James S. Donnelly, *The great Irish potato famine* (Stroud, 2002), p. 140.

13 Dictionary of Irish architects at http://www.dia.ie/works/view, accessed 29 Sept. 2011.

14 *Landed estate court rentals* (O' Brien) NAI microfilm, 39/1 24 June 1851.

15 *Belfast News-Letter*, 22 Nov. 1865.

16 Patrick Netterville to Joshua McEvoy Netterville, 28 Nov. 1865 (NLI, Synnott Papers, microfilm, p7219).

17 Ibid.

18 David Synnott, 'Marcella Gerrard's estate', *Journal of the Galway Archaeological and Historical Society*, 33 (1985), 43.

19 Patrick Netterville to Joshua McEvoy Netterville, 5 Dec. 1865 (NLI, Synnott papers, microfilm, p7219).

20 Ibid.

21 Ibid.

22 Patrick Netterville to Joshua McEvoy Netterville, 6 Jan. 1866 (NLI, Synnott papers, microfilm, p7219).

23 *Roscommon Messenger*, 23 Dec. 1865.

24 Ibid.

25 Patrick Netterville to Joshua McEvoy Netterville, 6 Jan. 1866 (NLI, Synnott papers, microfilm, p7219).

26 Ibid.

27 Patrick Netterville to Joshua McEvoy Netterville, 26 Feb. 1866 (NLI, Synnott papers, microfilm, p7219).

28 *Galway Vindicator*, 28 Mar. 1866.

29 Ibid.

30 *Roscommon Journal*, 31 Mar. 1866.

31 Ibid.

32 *Minutes of evidence taken from the committee for privileges to whom the petition of James Netterville Esquire, of Frahane, to his majesty, claiming the title, dignity and honour of Viscount Netterville of the kingdom of Ireland*, (206), HL, 1830, cclxxviiii, pp 44–51.

33 Manuscript copy, will of Edmond Netterville, 15 Nov. 1765, and codicil attached, 11 Apr. 1776 (NAI, 999/658/1).

34 *Roscommon Journal*, 31 Mar. 1866.

35 Ibid.

36 U. Hussey De Burgh, *The landowners of Ireland: an alphabetical list of the owners of estates of 500 acres or £500 valuation* (Dublin, 1878), pp 152, 336 & 511.

37 Gerard P. Moran, *Sir Robert Gore Booth and his landed estate in County Sligo, 1814–1876* (Dublin, 2006), p. 34.

38 Minutes, board of guardians, Mount Bellew Poor Law Union, 4 Sept. 1852, (Archives, Galway county library).

39 *Census of Ireland for the years 1901 and 1911*, NAI, accessed on line, http://census.nationalarchives.ie, 7 Oct. 2011.

40 Bridget Mitchell to her niece, 9 June 1908, copy in the author's possession.

41 John Fallon's account of encounter with Cloughbrack tenants, 11 June 1874 (NAI, private acquisitions, 999/658/11).

42 Ejectment decree for overholding, Arthur James Viscount Netterville v Ardeevan tenants (NAI, 999/658/1).

CONCLUSION

1 James S. Donnelly Jr, 'Landlords and tenants' in W.E. Vaughan (ed.), *A new history of Ireland: v, Ireland under the Union, 1801–70* (Oxford, 1989), p. 341.

2 NAI, Private acquisitions collection, 999/658/10.

3 NAI, Private acquisitions collection, 999/658/11.

4 *Galway Express*, 13 June 1879.